IT'S A STATE OF MIND

STOP EXISTING | START LIVING

JAMES BOARDMAN

LET'S TELL YOUR STORY PUBLISHING

LONDON

COPYRIGHT

This book is dedicated to my children Angelina, Alba and Bailey, who in my darkest hour saved my life

CONTENTS

ACKNOWLEDGEMENTS

Massive thanks go to my partner Jemima and my children, Angelina, Alba and Bailey, for their patience while I dedicated time to writing this book.

Thanks for putting up with me day in and day out Jemima, and always supporting and guiding me in the right direction.

Massive thanks to my ma. She had it tough bringing me up without my dad and has got me this far.

Massive thanks to my circle for their constant and honest opinions on my ideas, my well-being from working too much and for their friendship that means the world.

Massive thanks to all my clients who trust me with their fitness, health and lifestyle.

Massive thanks to Ricky Knight, who has spent the last year helping me develop my business and my understanding of the industry. Without this knowledge and accountability I would not be where I am today.

Massive thanks to Dan Meredith, who helped me understand the entrepreneurial world and whose resources in Espresso With Dan have helped me understand exactly what it takes to be successful online.

Last but by no means least, massive thanks to Colette Mason, who has been an amazing coach – supporting me, guiding me and scaring me with her accountability.

INTRODUCTION

ABOUT ME

Hi, I'm James Boardman.

I have three children, Bailey Angelina and another little lady Alba, who is just two weeks old as I write. Without a doubt, my children saved my life. Their presence and love brought me back from the depths of despair and depression, and they won't realise that until they are older.

I have a wonderful partner in Jemima, who is looking forward to being a mummy and who supports me through everything I do.

I live in the South East of England. I've travelled in small doses but nothing like what I want to.

I'm an ambitious 38-year-old guy, who wants to help as many people as possible to be the best version of themselves.

My mission is to touch as many lives as I can, to make a difference in people's thinking and to raise self-awareness in everyone's daily actions.

I proudly served in the Royal Marines for just over eight years, which gave me focus at a point in my life when I needed it.

I had no qualifications or direction until I watched the war film Black Hawk Down and thought it would be an amazing idea to join up!

Becoming a Royal Marine Physical Trainer (PTIRM) was one of the proudest moments in my career. It was something that I looked at in the brochure at the very start and wanted to be.

I was also told it was never going to happen because it's so tough to get in, but I fucking proved them all wrong. I have a habit of doing that.

It was simply the best job I've ever had and miss the role I played; like an ex-girlfriend you fell for heavily then split from.

Back in "Civvy Street", my life is now very different. I have a lot to contend with!

Running my company, Bodyshock Fitness, is my new career. It was launched 3½ years ago and there are more than 250 people who regularly turn up for my classes each week. Then there's the 100-plus online clients working on my programmes to develop themselves.

After that, I have eight personal clients to take care of at any one time as well!

Of course my life has its challenging days, but I love to help people. No matter how busy it gets, I always strive to provide a service that far exceeds client expectations.

Being a business owner is demanding. Those of you reading who run your own company will know what I'm talking about. Stresses and anxieties all come into play. Perhaps, like me, you find it's so difficult to switch off, especially if your office is currently in your dining room.

I'm an extremely ambitious, highly-driven chap and work could easily take over my life. Balancing my lifestyle so that it isn't dominated by work is tough and I have to be on my game each day to cope.

Without a doubt, bringing up my three kids is harder than anything I've ever done, especially as they get older. I'm already finding myself worrying that I'm not going to see them for much longer. They'll soon hit that stage where they are too "grown up" to want to hang out with dad anymore.

My kids are my world. As a dad of three, I have my hands full for the foreseeable future.

If all of that wasn't enough to deal with, I have the stresses of moving to a bigger home to contend with this year. There is no avoiding it; as a family have simply outgrown the current one.

When we are settled in, I'm planning to have a dedicated office with more space. I am sure this will help me manage my work/life balance.

As you can see my life is busy, but I like it that way. How do I survive? I rely heavily on planning and I'll teach you my system in this book.

MY DARKEST HOUR

It was around 1am and I was lying awake in the family home by myself. I had driven my family away, I had left my job in the Marines and I had no identity. I was in a deep depression, but didn't realise it at the time.

I had no real friends as I had spent the last eight years away from my home town, so had no connections.

I didn't know what to do. I was suffocated by the person that I had become. I had to find the old me again, break the cocoon and get out.

At the time I didn't know what else to do other than go for a run. So that's what I did, I went for a run. A 30-minute run turned into an hour run, an hour run turned into two hours and so on. I ended up running for three hours. I hadn't run in months. I hadn't done any fitness in months because I couldn't be arsed – I was too busy trying to figure my shit out. I had been in prime condition as a physical trainer in the Marines but by now I was out of shape.

> That run changed my whole perspective of life. I thought about what was important in my life. What was I going to do? What was I good at?
>
> I'm a big believer in fate, and I believe that I was meant to go on that run in order to reflect on my life. I thought so hard about things that I lost track of time. I came back with a plan and a reminder what my "why" was. I knew what I had to do and set about getting it done.

I had no help back then, no self-awareness of what I was doing or the position I was in. Sometimes you need a shake – a kick up the arse – and that's what this book is. So read it, wake up and smell the roses – it's time to reclaim your life.

WHY I WROTE THIS BOOK

Have you noticed the thousands, in fact millions, of men over the age of 35 struggling to get through each day. They come from every walk of life – from builders to company directors, professional sportsmen to Sunday league footballers.

Why are they struggling? Why are *you* struggling? Somewhere along the way you got lost or stuck in a rut. Many men have lost touch with their true identity and struggle to find their purpose in this world.

The antidote to this is upgrading your mindset, increasing self-awareness and understanding what you want out of life.

Mindset is vital to the development of your life. It's the key to personal development, your health, your work or business, and your relationships.

When you have control and balance in each of these four categories, you can move forwards and live a life that brings enjoyment, fulfilment, health and prosperity.

This book will open your eyes about how your identity has evaporated over the years causing you anxiety, depression, low confidence and low self-esteem.

At times, I will be ruthless about where you may actually be in life and how you can turn things around – because when you've lost your mojo a big dose of tough love is the only way to snap out of it.

HOW MY SPARK GOT SNUFFED OUT

I began my career in the Royal Marines as a sniper.

I passed my sniper course and was deployed to Afghanistan in January 2006. I started working as part of a six-man team to protect the Royal Engineers.

After two years of being a sniper I had the opportunity to become a Royal Marine Physical Trainer, which I snapped up and qualified in 2008. Being in the forces was the most amazing job for me, even to date.

Working with recruits – watching them turn up as boys (shitting themselves) and then turning them into men trained to defend this country – was an honour.

I worked with some of the most inspiring and awesome guys around and it was a privilege to know them.

I guess I see my role now as being similar – helping men struggling in life to turn things round and develop no matter what level they are at.

September 26th, 2011, was the date I left the Royal Marines. I remember driving back home with one consuming thought: "Have I done the right thing?"

What made me leave if I loved it so much? I wanted to be at home with my family to be a full-time dad. Seeing them at weekends just didn't cut it.

Looking back, my transition from military to civilian life was all of 48 hours. I left working with highly-motivated recruits in the Royal Marines, to teaching teenagers aged 16 to 18 at a local college. And the worst thing was that they didn't want to be there.

For the first 12 months it was very apparent to me that I was changing and not in a good way. I was failing as a husband, a father, a friend and as an employee.

I was failing in life.

I had lost any ambition, spark, identity and vision of where my life was going.

I had a job I didn't want to be in and found no satisfaction from the role. I was broke, on the bones of my arse, because I had taken a £10,000 pay cut to move back 'home'.

I found it difficult to go from a job that gave me pride, ambition, identity and drive – to becoming stuck in a dead-end job that was quite the opposite. This was tough to deal with.

Everyone is capable of achieving amazing things. For you, this may seem like a long way off from your current situation. However, it isn't out of your reach.

Recapturing your best is a state of mind. I chose to put this book together as a tool to help you realise that. Open up your eyes to the things stopping you and holding you back. I wanted to share a way forward for you to be able see your path, plan and implement, and be the best version of yourself.

I went through a very difficult time in my life. It was very lonely and hard to accept, and I had made an awful lot of mistakes along the way.

I never really dealt with the depression or anxiety I felt. I just kind of 'got on with it'. At the time I didn't understand. I went from having a love for life to falling into a rut that I couldn't get out of. I imagine that if you are reading this book you may be in a similar position.

My hope is that this book puts some spice back into your life. I hope that the journey I took helps you realise that you are not the only man in the world that feels the way you do.

I don't want you to be stuck in that hellish rut for years. I want to drag you out of that state of mind and help you to build a winning mentality.

WHO THIS BOOK IS FOR

This book is aimed at men over the age of 35 who want to improve the way they live their lives. It looks at the problems men face as we get older.

Lack of direction is a common problem.

I've worked alongside men in their 30s and 40s who are directors of big companies; men who thought they had clear direction in their life, only to wake up one day and find out that they didn't, and that they were just lying to themselves.

Direction can apply to many things – family life, relationships, health or business for example. This book is for those who are tired and fed up of feeling in limbo and who need to work on a clear vision of where they are going.

Moving forward takes a chain reaction from having no direction, to having an idea of a plan, to implementing that plan, and then to building momentum and consistency.

This book helps you to establish a solid strategy and thought process using proven tactics to move forwards and achieve the life you want and deserve.

Many men feel trapped in different ways. This can be through not reaching their full potential, treading water in dead-end relationships, being tied into a job they hate just to keep the roof over their head, or not being confident enough to go to the gym.

You will explore the emotion of feeling trapped and how you can break down the mental prison. You can move forwards with your life, and be free from the feelings of fear, anxiety, self-doubt or low self-esteem.

Now you finally feel the time is right, that time when you decide to do something about moving yourself forward, this book will guide you through.

As you look for inspiration, this book will enable you audit your life, to draw a line in the sand, so you are in a position to act. It is certainly going to make you be honest with yourself.

WHAT THIS BOOK COVERS

This book uncovers the deep issues that are preventing you from living the life you want to. You will look at the various triggers that can cause you stress and frustration. It will draw out emotion and help you to look at your life from an honest perspective.

It looks in detail at proven methods that will take you from a chaotic lifestyle that lacks routine to a way of living that finds everyday balance.

It teaches you to put together a concrete plan and be more proactive. You will learn about the power of habits and routines, and build the structure you need to move forwards.

Let's look at each chapter in turn.

HOW YOU GET TO ROCK BOTTOM AND WHAT IT MEANS

Men approaching 35 and beyond are likely to go through physical and mental changes. The introduction of new and bigger responsibilities is likely to change the way you live your life.

The days of doing what you like, when you like, have gone. You now have demands to deal with in your work and family life that will restrict your freedom to be the free spirit you might have once been. For some, that restriction brings the change of mind and body, which can be overwhelming and hard to deal with, and they hit what feels like rock bottom.

Maybe it's consistently lying to yourself about where you are in life? Are you drinking in the evening to numb the frustration and the unhappiness?

For most men who find themselves in this position, the fire in their belly has gone. The drive has gone. They feel they've lost their purpose and they can't carry on like that much longer.

It's time to turn things around. It's time to face some hard facts about the way you have been living your life. It's time to start self-auditing and making a plan of action. You are going to look deeply at yourself. To move forwards you must first confront the past and present.

To do that, I am going to ask you to use your gut instinct to score four key areas in your life out of ten. Once you've finished this chapter and audited your life, you will know what is going well for you and what isn't. It's an uncomfortable truth, but it will spur you on to make positive changes.

WHAT FACTORS RAISE OR LOWER YOUR AUDIT SCORE

Having a long, hard look at yourself and what you have become is often a difficult process to understand and accept.

There are usually many feelings of anger for allowing things to get as bad as they have.

Sometimes men feel ashamed at how they have let themselves go or feel upset that they haven't been prioritising what matters most. You will read about how to face those feelings and deal with them in the right way. Believe it or not, you are massively winning by coming to terms with what you find.

Once you know more about how a variety of factors can improve or diminish the quality of your life, I want to you review the four key areas again – looking in detail at the cold hard facts of what's actually working and what's not, rather than your initial gut instinct.

I promise you'll find some pleasant surprises among some of the disappointments when you do your second assessment.

GETTING BACK ON TRACK

In this chapter, it's time to look at how to make sense of what's going on and start to think about a better plan for the future.

You'll start by considering how well you have done by facing up to the problems you need to solve. Then I will share with you the power of planning and teach you how to set better priorities to guide you towards a more fulfilling life.

The chapter closes with assessing your audit to see what the biggest problems are so you can put a plan in place to solve them as quickly as possible. Once you know what you definitely want to focus on, you can put together a detailed plan, which is covered in the next section.

HOW TO CREATE PLAN TO MOVE FORWARDS

Now you understand your situation, what's working and what's not, it's time to start moving forwards.

You look at how introducing positive habits, routines and structure to your life are the ways to win.

I will teach you how to put together yearly, 12-week, weekly and daily plans. These will add structure to your life, so you can take control of what you do and how you do it. The plans give you a destination to aim for and a tool for making sure you consistently work towards being the person you want to become.

Once you know how to make improvements, the next step is learning how to do those consistently to get the best results.

HOW TO MAKE LIFE-LONG CHANGES SUCCESSFULLY

Once you learn how to plan, you need to know how to stick with it in the long term. You will learn important lessons to maintain your progress. You will be introduced to the CICR formula. This stands for

- **C**ommitment
- **I**mplementation
- **C**onsistency
- **R**eview/rethink

You will master the techniques to keep growing as an individual, how to always improve yourself and to be the best version of yourself – now and in the future.

WHAT TO DO AFTER YOUR FIRST 12-WEEK PLAN

The last chapter of the book talks about not falling back into your bad old habits.

I'm sure you've made bold New Year's resolutions in the past, only to see them fade into obscurity a few weeks later. I am going to teach you how to stick with your objectives for life.

I'll also give you some advice on how to put together subsequent plans.

HOW TO USE THIS BOOK

The first time you read this book, you are probably going to feel like you've been hit by a truck. Facing up to the cold, hard truth is a lot to deal with mentally.

You have to read the information from the start to the finish to fully grasp the process you need to follow. If you skip through chapters, you will miss important steps you need to understand. As you go, mark paragraphs that you can relate to the most. This is good for quick reference in future.

I've included my own stories and some from my clients to prove it's not just you who has become lost or overwhelmed – and that there is an answer. I know a lot of people take comfort in knowing it's not just them having these struggles, and that other people's insights can be highly motivating.

I have set some tasks for you. There are two types of task:

- exercises to audit your life and your take on where you are now, and what makes life worth living
- planning sessions to put a system in place so you focus on what needs to be done to make you happy again

I have created a downloadable, worked example of a completed plan so that you can clearly see the sort of information to include in your own plan, and how much detail you need to go into. You can find it in the resources section.

If you want to connect with other guys working hard to transform their lives, I run a free Facebook group called JB Men's Group. It is for those men that want to hold themselves publicly accountable and share their experiences with others travelling on the same path.

If you have a question, you can email me any time at:

me@boardmanjames.com.

THE PLANNING PROCESS

1.	Carry out a gut instinct review of your life
2.	Do a detailed audit of how things are going
3.	Review what's working and what's not, brainstorm solutions
4.	Set your yearly goals
5.	Create your 12-week plan
6.	Create your weekly plan for week one
7.	Create your daily plan for week one (optional)
8.	Follow your first week and review it
9.	Plan the next 11 weeks
10.	Follow the plan for the remaining weeks
11.	Take a week off to assess
12.	Plan the next 12 weeks

LET'S GO

Congratulations on taking the first steps to changing your life. It's not easy to admit to yourself you're in a bad place.

It's often hard dealing with changes in your life, but I want to help. I want the best for you. I want to see the very best version of you come to the fore.

You have some testing times ahead, facing up to some of the realities of your current situation.

However, if you follow the advice in this book right through to the end I can promise you that you will be much happier, more confident and able to move forward with your life.

HOW DID YOU GET TO ROCK BOTTOM

Can you remember when it all started to feel wrong for you? When your life didn't feel like your own anymore? There may have been a specific event in your life or you might have just drifted into it.

Whatever the reason, the main thing now is to focus on making some bold changes to reclaim your life!

In this first chapter, I am going to explain how daily life can become a real grind.

Then it's time to make a start on planning your new life.

You'll begin by using your gut instinct to assess how your life is going.

You will become clear on which specific areas of your day-to-day life you are struggling with.

We'll build on this idea in the second chapter when I'll explain what can raise or lower your quality of life, followed by a deeper look into what's going on in your life.

LET'S AUDIT YOUR LIFE

Accepting where you are right now is a brutal process, but a necessary one to enable you to progress.

Have you ever sat down, had a good think about how things are going and written it all down? If you haven't, don't worry – few people bother to do this.

Have you ever wondered how many men over the age of 35 are on autopilot, simply drifting through life, putting up with the way they are, and expecting that 'one day' they will do something about it?

Does this sound familiar?

I'll start tomorrow...

I'll start Monday...

Denial is like a 10ft wall blocking your path.

Denial leads to a lack of action, stress, unhealthy and out-of-shape bodies, unhappy relationships, and a sense of gloom about career choices.

What if you could learn to self-audit your behaviours and habits? Armed with that information, you can begin to take action to move forwards with your life.

Breaking life down into four key areas has been a good foundation for looking at how I am doing and what needs to be better.

These areas are:

- personal development
- health
- professional life
- relationships

Let me explain the benefit of analysing these four areas.

EVERY JOURNEY NEEDS A STARTING POINT

Have a think about taking a long journey in the car or on a train. There's a set process to follow to make sure you get to your destination, isn't there? Typically, it will be:

- identifying a good reason to travel
- planning a route
- buying fuel or a ticket
- packing the right kit
- bringing the right people
- having the right tools, like a sat nav and your wallet

What will you need to take a new route in your life?

Guidance?

Motivation?

A plan?

By looking at your life and identifying the areas that you want to improve (i.e. your destination), you can start planning and adjusting your route to smooth the way.

Self-auditing means you'll know what you will do to make the improvements needed to get the result you want – in this case, a life worth living (rather than a train ticket to Edinburgh...).

Your new life all starts with writing this stuff down.

Instead of the whirling thoughts in your head constantly wearing you down, you can liberate yourself from a lot of the pain with a simple pen and paper.

Be bold with your notes, don't hold back. The more truthful you are the better the self-evaluation.

You will find that once you start writing things down more, things will creep into your head and you will start identifying issues you may have not given much thought to in the past. It's like one big clear out; emptying your mind of all those dark thoughts.

You will feel like a weight has been lifted off your shoulders after the process.

IT'S TIME TO REFLECT ON THE TRUTH

Get up feeling tired, drag yourself to work, deal with problem after problem, come home, collapse on the sofa, have a few beers and maybe a takeaway, watch some TV and then go to sleep – only to wake up and repeat it all the next day.

Does this sound like your life?

It feels like Groundhog Day, right?

How much time do you dedicate to boosting your wellbeing in a day or a week?

I mean 'you' time with no phones, computers and no family, just you?

How often do you sit down with a coffee and think about how your life is going?

Are you aware of your bad habits or bad moods? Do you know what your strengths are? Are you reactive or proactive?

Although you may not realise it, you review things all the time. For example, when you come out of the cinema the first thing you talk about with the people you went with was what you all thought of the film.

What else might people review?

Let's take football for example. You probably know somebody that thinks they should be a Premier League manager. They think they could do a much better job of everything – picking the team, killer tactics on the pitch, buying new players. When they review a performance of their favourite team, they tell you all about how it should have been done in great detail! They talk about the system, the players used and whether it worked or not. They know what went wrong and whose fault it was. They will do this with passion.

How many times have you reviewed what's working – or not – in your life with the same rigour?

No football team would improve without reviewing their performance after a game. The same is true for you and your life.

It's time now for you to dip your toe in the water and start reviewing your life!

TASK: DO YOUR LIFE AUDIT

What you need to do

I want you to look at four areas in your life and rate them out of ten. The areas are:

- personal development
- health
- business
- relationships

And like the armchair football manager, you'll use these scores to review how you're doing. Some sections have more than one score, such health and relationships. Use the average for your final score for those areas.

Why you should audit your life

Scoring the key areas in your life helps you keep track of what's going on and where you're heading.

The answers you get will help you to prioritise and build structure into your life to make the improvements you need to. Having no structure makes you like a boat with no sail. You will not move forwards. You will drift aimlessly, buffeted by the wind and waves, and with no clear direction.

How to do the audit

Read the descriptions below for each of the four areas and then go through the questions. When assessing your situation, base your score on the last year of your life.

Give a score out of 10 for each, with 10 the highest and one the lowest. Don't bullshit – you will only be lying to yourself, which will do you no good at all.

PERSONAL DEVELOPMENT

During your school years you develop knowledge and skills. You learn through social interaction, lessons and your teachers. Some go on to college and university to learn even more.

Personal development is about developing your knowledge, skills and understanding within a particular subject.

For example: if you struggle with anxiety and low self-esteem, which self-help books have you read in the last 12 months to help solve those problems?

You could be learning things like

- new software packages at work to boost your chance of promotion
- which foods you enjoy that help you lose weight
- actionable ideas from others by reading or listening to a podcast

As well as picking up new skills in any discipline, many people find developing their knowledge in self-help enables them to deal with stress more easily.

It improves coping mechanisms and, in the long run, helps them make better choices in life. Personal development is an excellent way to open up your imagination to new opportunities. It builds your confidence and helps you to grow.

When scoring yourself, look at how much you have developed as a person in the past year.

My personal development score out of 10 is ___

HEALTH

Eating and drinking

Most people think they are eating well. When I ask a client what their eating habits are like, they say "good". But when I look at their food diary and fluid intake it's really not "good" at all.

Ask yourself questions like, do you

- eat lots of fresh food or junk food and takeaways
- commit to following a food programme
- stick with a nutrition plan
- drink more pints of beer than water every week

For many of us, eating habits crumble because of the structure of our day – always so reactive and chaotic. How many times do you actually plan and prepare your meals and snacks for the next day or week?

The benefit of spending time getting your meals planned and ready is that you are able to control exactly what you eat, rather rely on unhealthy snacks and take-outs.

My eating and drinking score out of 10 is ___

Exercise

Are you doing all you can to stay in shape or have you become a couch potato? Are you being active in making a positive impact to your body and mind?

Don't score yourself based on the thoughts and wants you put into exercising, but what you actually do now! Remember, there is a distinct difference between saying and doing.

No bullshitting, right?

My exercise score out of 10 is ___

My overall health score out of 10 is ___

PROFESSIONAL LIFE

Adults spend the majority of their time involved with their work and career. Do you enjoy what you do? What would you do if you followed your passion? There are two ways to score your career depending on if you are employed in a job or self-employed and running your own business.

If you are employed

You spend most of your time thinking about work or working. So, when you give yourself a score consider the following:

- does it make you happy
- are you satisfied in your job
- does it consume your life

I know you can't just go out and do whatever you want career-wise. I'm not naive enough to think you don't have bills to pay or a mortgage to clear.

But, have you ever sat and looked at the bigger picture, and asked yourself the questions above? How do you really feel about what you're doing? In the longer term, a career change is a distinct possibility.

My employed career score out of 10 is ___

If you are self-employed

Have a think about these factors if you are self-employed or run a business

- how motivated are you
- are you giving it everything
- are you working in or on your business
- does it bring in the rewards you deserve
- do you enjoy it

When you evaluate yourself and your business, you are likely to open up some truths and gaps in your business.

Again, it is trying to get into the habit of looking at areas of your life that need attention so you can improve – so be honest!

My self-employed career score out of 10 is __

RELATIONSHIPS

When you see the word "relationship" you'll probably first think about your partner. When you do this exercise, it's important to widen your perspective. Think about the relationship you have with your

- children
- siblings
- parents
- friends
- professional connections

How well do you manage those relationships? Where are you lacking?

Partner

How well are you communicating with your partner? In truth, if you are not looking at your partner as your support, your 'rock', then you have to start asking questions. (I'm no relationship counsellor; I'm just giving honest views from my perspective.)

A lot of unhappiness stems from poor relationships with partners. If you are around a negative influence, then it's likely to affect your mood, which will in turn affect your mindset.

But if you have a happy relationship with your partner, it's the foundation for you to achieve everything you want. It makes the world of difference when your partner has got your back.

My partner score out of 10 is __

Family

Let's think about children, brothers, sisters, parents. Are you spending enough time with them all? Do your children get your full attention or only half because you work while they sit patiently waiting for you to take a break? If you have kids and you are doing that, maybe you get that gnawing feeling of guilt – that's what I felt when I used to do it.

How often are you keeping in touch with your parents or your siblings? Do you drift in and out of each other's lives as and when, or is there a strong bond?

My family score out of 10 is __

Friendships

Now, there are best mates and then your wider circle of friends. What's important to understand with friendships is what they think of you? Do they think you're a good friend? Do you do enough for them, to make sure they're OK? If I were to ask them what type of friend you are, what would they say?

If you want a quick mood booster, message someone right now and tell them how much you value what they bring to your life.

My friendships score out of 10 is __

Professional connections

This is an interesting one. If you are a manager of people, what's the relationship like with your staff? What would they say about you?

If you are an employee, what's the relationship like with your colleagues and boss?

If you are a business owner, how well do you connect with others? What's the relationship like with your clients? Do you value them enough?

Professional relationships can be vital to the growth of your business, your chances of promotion or how enjoyable your time at work can be. How are you doing?

My professional connections score out of 10 is ___

My average relationship score out of 10 is ___

MY LIFE AUDIT SCORES

Jot down all your scores for easy reference. Remember to put the average for health and relationship scores.

- ___ personal development
- ___ health
  - ___ eating and drinking
  - ___ exercise
- ___ professional life
- ___ relationships
  - ___ partner
  - ___ children
  - ___ family
  - ___ friendships
  - ___ professional connections

Now you have your scores it's time to learn more about the factors that can raise or lower them. This information will help you pinpoint the areas that need attention.

FACTORS AFFECTING YOUR AUDIT SCORE

You have completed your audit and may well be thinking, "oh shit" when you see your low scores.

But don't lose heart. Remember that the point of the life audit is to start fixing these things and to do that properly, you need to see where you are right now.

It's time to learn how so many men end up feeling bitter and twisted about their life, and if things really are as gloomy as they might seem based on your gut instinct assessment.

Over the years, I have found quite a lot of men struggle to find out what really drives them in life – their "*why*", their "*purpose*" – so there's a task to help you make sense of that if you can't put yours into words any more.

Once you've read this chapter, I want you to reassess your life audit scores to see if you still agree with the instinctive ratings you gave or if you want to make some revisions (either up or down) in the light of this new information.

It is crucial you are honest with your review. No bullshitting. Denial is one of the things causing your pain right now.

Let's have a look at a series of things that can influence your scores.

YOUR ACTIONS NOT MATCHING YOUR PRIORITIES

What are the top five priorities in your life right now? What is it that really matters to you? Do it in your head or write it down.

My priorities in life...

1. _____
2. _____
3. _____
4. _____
5. _____

Done it?

Now ask yourself if that list *really* reflects what's going on in your life. Are you putting effort into those things, or have they fallen by the wayside?

Remember no denial and no false truths. Be honest to yourself!

For example, if family or relationships are top of your priority list, are you

- leaving on time to be home for a family dinner or staying late at work
- talking to each other at the restaurant rather than staring at your phones
- focusing on understanding your partner and their needs or are you second guessing
- paying attention to the children over the weekend or being distracted about the week ahead

If family is genuinely your priority, then they should be item number one in real life, not in your hopes and dreams.

I want you to have another go, and write out your real list of priorities based on what's going on from day to day, where your time, effort and focus are going. It might be hard to write down the truth when it triggers feelings of guilt, failure and anger that you are not prioritising the things that matter most, but you need to do it. Being in denial is what brought you to where you are.

What I am actually doing with my time and effort...

1. _____

2. _____

3. _____

4. _____

5. _____

Are the things that matter near the top of your revised list? Or have your "obligations" taken over?

You are in charge of your life and you can make a plan to put things right if they have gone out of kilter. The good news is you're making positive steps towards that life already by being more aware about why things are not running the way you want them to be.

CONSTANTLY PUTTING OTHERS NEEDS ABOVE YOURS

Let's talk about you for a second. When it comes to looking after your wellbeing and your health, where are you at? I know most mums often prioritise their children above themselves and it's one of the reasons mothers so special.

But what about you? Are you looking after number one?

Where so many people go wrong is by always prioritising others rather than concentrating on themselves.

Don't get me wrong, it's a bloody good thing to be there for others – but not at the long-term sacrifice of yourself and your own development.

What good are you to others if you are burnt out and fed up because you're not looking after *you*?

 Some people often feel guilty or selfish for putting themselves first. It feels wrong. If that idea strikes a chord with you, just remember those aeroplane safety announcements – "put your oxygen mask on first before helping those around you". It's the right thing to do.

If your current priorities make you feel tired, frustrated or angry because you've lost sight of what needs to happen to make you happy then you are going to find life more difficult.

Could this be the reason why you are not winning with your health? A lot of men say, "Yeah mate, I'm gonna smash it up, I'm on it" – and then the excuses creep in and nothing gets done. Other things take over.

Imagine if a year ago you committed to training three times a week. Think about where you would be right now. Think about the benefits to your body, which would in turn build your confidence, which in turn helps combat anxiety and depression – the benefits are endless.

Imagine if you backed up everything you said you were going to do with action – made it a priority – how would life be then?

DO YOU PUT OFF DOING THINGS FOR YOU?

As a young boy, I remember reading a book about doing something today so that you didn't have to do it tomorrow. It was a book I never forgot simply because of the message.

If I did the washing up tonight, it would be done. I wouldn't waste time thinking, 'Oh, no, I've got to do that tomorrow'. If I tidied my room today, I wouldn't waste time thinking, 'Oh, no, I've got to do that tomorrow'. Who wants those gloomy thoughts circling round in their head all the time?

That book taught me the benefit of taking action and responsibility to improve my life, rather than spinning my wheels, feeling fed up and frustrated – with nothing but problems to occupy my mind.

Every time I have to do something, even writing this book, I think back to that simple lesson.

If I write just one more chapter, that's another chapter down. I can start a new one tomorrow.

So my question to you is: What do you put off? What have you said you would do but never backed it up with action?

(I have my hand up... ME! For so long I did this; got pumped up and said I would do something only to not follow through.)

One thing I did was start up a daily video diary on YouTube.

It was something I committed to doing every day, no matter what. Much like the armchair football pundit, it's also given me an opportunity to review my days and actions, and learn to become the best version of myself.

YOUR BODY REFLECTS HOW LOW DOWN "YOU" ARE IN YOUR PRIORITIES

If you have an injury or a debilitating illness that prevents you from getting in shape, this process won't necessarily relate to you – but it does for everyone else.

If you stood in front of the mirror right now in your underwear and reviewed your body shape, it will most likely reflect how much you prioritise yourself.

If you are overweight, unfit, and unhappy, no one has put a gun to your head and told you to choose that life. You are responsible for every action that you take; every decision.

It's hard hitting, that reflection in the mirror. It may trigger some anger and frustration. (If you were looking for some fluffy words then this is the wrong book.)

Don't roll your eyes and sigh deeply. Don't tell me that you don't have time or "It's alright for you, James". (By the time this book is published, I will have three children including a newborn. I run four businesses and look after nearly 500 clients. If I manage to find 60 minutes a day, then so can you!)

You might have told yourself that you don't have time to dedicate to your health and wellbeing. Well, I think that's a poor excuse! I am calling you out on your bullshit.

Here's something to try that will give you some space in your day to focus on your priorities.

THE 'GOLDEN HOUR'

The golden hour is an hour each day that is set aside to be your time. No phones. No computers. Nothing. Just time for you and your wellness. Getting up an hour earlier works well, but you can choose any time that suits you.

As long as you can do it consistently at that time slot, that's fine. (If an hour feels like a lot to commit to right now, start with 30 minutes. The main thing is that you start doing this!)

The beauty of having a golden hour is that you now have time each day to concentrate on building new habits, routines and structure. It's a time when you can think about efficient ways to get things done – freeing up more time later on in the day or week.

It takes time to introduce these things and carry them out consistently, but they will benefit you and the way you live your life in the long run.

A LACK OF "YOU TIME"

"You time" provides a chance to reflect on how life is going. It's a time to enjoy yourself or to put together a plan to solve problems, rather than get overwhelmed with panicky firefighting.

It's a chance to listen to some songs you love that make you feel happy. It's a chance to read a chapter of the book you got for your birthday that you never got round to reading. You could do that 30-minute brisk walk while listening to a podcast.

TIP: Your golden hour is a great opportunity to have regular "you time".

A LACK OF A STRONG "WHY"

Why do you do anything? Why? It's a question I've often asked myself. Have you ever wondered exactly what a "why" is and how it is important to you and your development?

In a nutshell, your "why" is your driving motivation to do something. It's the reason you work hard at your job. It's the reason you go to the gym, make the effort in your relationships, or advance in your personal development.

When you don't feel motivated to do something, complete a goal or undertake a tedious task, the idea is that you think of your why to boost your motivation to get it done.

Are you focusing the stuff that genuinely matters to you versus the things that you are obliged to do? So much time and frustration is wasted on trying to achieve obligations, often for the benefit of others rather than you directly.

Do you feel the frustration and stress builds because you want to focus on the important things in life, but all your time gets lost in other commitments?

What actually matters to you?

It can be hard to understand your why. It is usually something that is going to be emotional, something that means an awful lot to you as a person. Personally, I work hard in my businesses because I want to provide for my growing family, to move into that bigger house we need.

These types of whys are the best because they are the ones that are going to give you the motivation to succeed. Whereas tick-the-box whys you do just for the sake of it are weak. For example, *I want to lose weight so I look good* is pretty ineffective. Recognising being unfit means you raise the chances of the Grim Reaper visiting you at an early age and will leave your family to fend for themselves is a much stronger motivating factor.

Try this next task if you feel vague about what your "why" is.

TASK: WORK OUT YOUR WHY

What you need to do

I want you to ask yourself some questions and see what your intuition tells you.

Why you need to do this

It's worth spending time working out what your true "why" is, otherwise it's hard to work out what matters in life and what your priorities should be.

How to work out your "why"

Relax and keep asking yourself five open questions that start with the word why and see where it leads you.

Five example questions you could ask yourself are

- why do you want to make a change in your life
- why do you want to be fitter and in shape
- why do you want to live a better lifestyle
- why do you want to reduce the risk of illness
- why is important to you and your family

You'll probably answer with "...because" and then give a reason. Ask yourself why you feel that way about the reason.

Peel back the layers to get to the root cause of why you are trying to better yourself. You might be surprised what you come up with for your motivation. This exercise is a real eye-opener.

Here's an example of how I find this works for clients. Their first response is to say something factual like, "I want to get fit" or "I want to have a better lifestyle". That's helpful, but what we really need to do is draw out the emotional 'why'.

For some people, a loved one has died at a young age due to ill-health and they miss them. This sort of emotional why is much more powerful than thinking, "I should be down the gym right now and not in the pub." It gives you a potent reason to change.

Try it with anything in your life. Work out what that powerful emotional driver is.

MAKE THE MOST OF YOUR 'WHY'

Once you know what your why is, it's important to consistently remind yourself of it.

Here are a few simple tips to do that.

Wall stickers signs

Big Post-it™ notes and A4-printed signs around the house are a great way to remind you of what you are trying to achieve. Write out five or six with your why and post them in places you see regularly such as the fridge, mirrors, bedside cabinet etc.

Desktop / smartphone wallpaper

Take a photo of that Post-it note with your why on and use it as your PC desktop or phone wallpaper.

You will always be using your phone and, most likely, your computer quite regularly too. It doesn't just have to be a picture of the Post-it; it could be a photo of your family or the car you really want. Make it relevant to what your 'why' is.

TELLING YOURSELF 'DON'T HAVE ENOUGH TIME'

The majority of people who are struggling in life say they "don't have time" to correct their problems. It's my pet hate. Apparently it's their reason why they can't do anything. The old quote, "There's no such thing as no time, just poor planning," has never been truer.

It's weird, people always seem to have time for a Netflix box set for their must-see show, but not to take steps to improve their life. Hmm...

What system do you use to allocate your time? How do you break down your months, weeks, days or hours?

Are you someone that isn't too fussed about how they use their time? Or, are you on the ball, aware of the time available and what needs to be done – someone who sets deadlines to make sure it happens?

Does your body shape reflect that amount of time you spend on it? Does your business or career reflect the amount of time you put into it? Does your marriage reflect your commitment? Are you giving your children and your family enough of your time?

Honestly?

It's the same for anything in your life.

A lot of this comes down to your self-awareness, commitment, consistency and planning of what you are doing during your 24 hours a day.

NO TIME FOR EXERCISE

You don't have to be a rocket scientist to understand that the more sedentary you are, the more likely you are to put weight on. Burning calories is a vital part of weight loss. So if you have an inactive, desk-based job then you are going to have to make an effort to find a way to burn those calories.

Sitting in an office all day or driving for hours on end can also make you feel lacklustre when it comes to being active.

Your body gets so used to just sitting in the office or car for the majority of your day. Perhaps choosing to climb a few flights of stairs rather than taking the lift can be the first step to a more active you.

The decisions you make to counter that sedentary lifestyle by exercising regularly will make the difference between risking an early death and enjoying a happy, healthy and active old age.

It's tough, not glamourous and takes hard work, especially if you've been inactive all day.

 At times like this it's so important to remember your "why" to help motivate you. Getting home after driving all day or being

stuck at a desk for eight hours, then mustering the motivation and energy to go to the gym or a fitness session is a lot easier when you focus on your why. Your why will pull you through.

TOO MANY OBLIGATIONS

As adults, there is no hiding from our obligations.

What are you obliged to do?

Is there a way you can still meet those obligations in a more time-efficient manner than you doing everything personally? For example, if you want to spend more time with your family, why not get someone else in to mow the lawn?

Why not do your food shopping online, so you can buy the same set of healthy basics you need each week at the click of a mouse, rather than laboriously doing it in person? (Plus you avoid the risk being tempted by the sweets or alcohol aisle.)

Could you just say "no" to some of those obligations? I am sure you could put the time to better use. Yes?

GOING WITH THE FLOW RATHER THAN BEING STRUCTURED

It's very easy to just *go with the flow*, and the majority of people do. How often do you wake up with no structure, no plan, and just ride out the day rather than being in control? If there is no structure, life can tend to become stressful and frustrating, because it's so much harder to get anything done.

(You'll remember I asked you about how you plan a long car or train journey – you decide what needs to happen, you don't just set off and hope for the best).

Let's quickly look at structure and how it helps you get what you want out of life.

Structure is one of those things that are hard to come by. Everyone appreciates structure. Many people strive for structure, certainty and results. And of course, it's easier said than done.

People have an idea of how their day is structured (if you can call it that) but a common setback is the implementation (getting stuff done) and review process of how well their life is working.

Perhaps you get as far as picturing a structured day in your mind, but thinking is as far as you get.

How often do you act out that mental dress rehearsal to get the result you want versus just going with the flow and becoming frustrated with the way you drift along yet again?

The less structure you have, the less time you have to be structured. It quickly becomes a vicious circle, lurching from one firefight to the next.

Your success will be determined with how structured you are. If you are failing at fitness because of your time management, it's because you are *not prioritising it in how you structure your life.*

Other people manage to juggle their responsibilities with their personal goals – why not you?

DOUG'S TIME-CONSTRAINT CONUNDRUM

My client Doug was barely coping with the programme we were working on together. He told me 'time constraints' were the main barrier. I didn't believe him.

After some thought, he got to the root of the problem. It was clear that there was no structure to his day. There was no time was set aside for food preparation or workouts. As a result, his health score was low.

Time he could have been using more productively was slipping through his fingers on random tasks not contributing to boosting his health. He was going with the flow and just bouncing off the walls.

By implementing some time to plan and structure his day, he was able to boost his efficiency and productivity.

This gave him time to complete workouts, prepare some healthy meals and increase his productivity at work so he could leave on time.

Doug spent as little as 20 minutes sat down with his diary working out what he had to *for a whole week.*

This allowed him to prioritise his to do list and put it into a timed structure.

He was then able to know what he was doing and what time, instead of drifting from one thing to another and missing out what needed to be done to get the life he wanted.

This simple 20-minute strategy session meant he took ownership of his day, week and life once more.

Setting structure is a simple as saying

- I'll get up 30 minutes earlier then I normally do for a workout
- I'll prepare my meals between 19.30-20.00 to ensure I don't panic buy or skip meals tomorrow

Following a simple structured routine like this Monday to Friday will improve your habits and give you the space you need to get important stuff done.

Structure allows you to use the day in full and have maximum productivity, which means it's much easier to get the results you want – no matter how busy you feel you might be.

COMMUTING IS NOT 'DEAD TIME'

"I could not believe how much time I was wasting commuting to classes, appointments, school runs. I worked out on average I was commuting around two hours a day. All that time wasted!" – Mark Noble

These are the exact words from a client I spent six weeks training and developing.

Time is a valuable commodity.

If you commute to work by car you will most probably listen to the radio, and the majority of us don't really take it in.

Have you ever thought about listening to a podcast? You can get so much value from listening to them – especially the personal development shows.

They have the power to make you think about the way you are living your life, the actions you are taking and to build self-awareness!

Do you travel by train?

Are you just admiring the view out of the window or worse, staring at the departure board seeing your train is delayed again? You could be listening to a podcast or reading a book in this time.

How many books do you read? Remember, reading is that thing you used to do at school to help your development. It's a great way to pass the time on a long train journey.

If you struggle with eating properly, why not get a book on healthy eating and learn about the subject?

I'll bet that over a period of four weeks, travelling to and from work Monday to Friday, you could learn a hell of a lot about nutrition or self-motivation or about that new software package you need to use at work.

My point is that this commuting time is just as valuable as other time slots – use it wisely.

POOR CHOICES OFTEN LEAD TO MORE POOR CHOICES

Making poor choices seems to be a common theme in today's society – poor food choices, poor relationship choices or poor business decisions. A lot of the decisions that you make are made without thought. They are often made in haste due to your emotional state at the time.

Here's an example: You wake up late. There's no time for breakfast, so you don't eat. You run around throwing the things you think you need for your day into your bag, hoping nothing gets forgotten. You hunt around for your car keys. Your phone's got eight per cent battery left. You swear under your breath. You didn't prepare lunch so it's the pit stop at the superstore for crisps, a tired-

looking sandwich, a chocolate bar and a warm can of fizzy pop. This will probably be it until you get in for dinner.

During the day you've probably had a pint of water if that. You come home, collapse on the sofa armed with a few beers to try and unwind as you dread doing it all again tomorrow.

Your partner shouts to you from another room and you shout back because you're too tired to get up and go and talk to them properly.

You can see from this example how poor choices tend to snowball –– it all comes home to roost.

There has to come a time when you come out of the bubble and start making better decisions and take responsibility for what you are doing.

Imagine a world where you take your time to think before you act. Where you think before queuing up for fast food at lunch four times a week and where you think about the consequences of drinking a few beers every night to drown out the sorrows over a long period of time.

If you add a touch of self-awareness to your thoughts, maybe you could make better choices in life. (Thanks to your audit and those truthful scores, this is a lot easier.)

Have you heard of the concept of the rule of five?

Here's how it works. Think about the last five decisions you made:

- what made you make those decisions
- what was your emotional state
- what were the consequences

Were these choices going to move you forwards or backwards? Lots to think about, right?

A lot of this comes down to your personal awareness.

Some decisions you make can cause frustration, pain or stress, which all have a knock-on effect elsewhere in your life. The good news is just like bad decisions can snowball, good decisions can boost your progress towards the life you do want. You can build momentum.

If you can think about the poor decisions you make and why you make them, you will be one step closer to avoiding that situation next time.

Work out what needs to happen for you to make good decisions consistently.

MAKE TIME FOR GOOD DECISIONS

As I've explained, most people live in a reactive world. It's like the hamster wheel running round and round and the hamster's getting nowhere. They make hasty decisions based on their emotional state and never allow themselves time to think about long-term solutions.

In a world that is running at 200mph, where is your pit stop? Where can you take time out to assess the way your life's going, to review the decisions you're making, or fine tune your setup?

Very few get to do or practice this.

It doesn't happen overnight. You don't suddenly become good at this skill. I say it's a skill because learning to have time for yourself is a skill, a habit, a routine and part of a structure.

LIFE IN A BUBBLE

I picture the world as millions of people in their own little bubble. Every now and then, you have to come out of that bubble to see the bigger picture.

Every time you're in your bubble you only see what's in front of you and can only react to what's happening in that space.

But by coming out of it you can see everything that's happening and your vision becomes so much clearer.

This gives you to space you need to make good decisions.

Don't have time? Please don't tell yourself that. It's an excuse to escape accountability. Everyone has 60 minutes to themselves – even if it's on your commute – so get out of that bubble and smell the roses.

 Remember the idea of the golden hour? This is a fantastic opportunity for you to step outside your bubble, get off the merry-go-round for a moment, and make some better decisions.

COMMIT TO YOUR GOOD DECISIONS

If and when you do make a decision, do you commit to it? I bet you've set some New Year's resolutions and they were abandoned just two weeks into January, right?

For many people, half of the challenge is being committed and disciplined. At the end of a workday, when the guys invite you for a beer, you can either honour your decision to go home, prepare your food for tomorrow and spend time with your family or let peer pressure hold you back. Remember your commitment.

When the guys know you've chosen not to drink, do they support you or make jokes at your expense?

It's going to be hard for you to stick to your commitment when peer pressure is involved. You know when the boys are rounding up for a big night and all you want to do is get out there and have fun. Do you stick or bust?

How about weekends?

As soon as the weekend arrives, it changes your routine if you work Monday to Friday. Now you have time on your hands – time that challenges your discipline and resolve. The same applies for shift workers. Temptations raise their ugly head.

Downtime means there's often too much time to think about things that aren't going so well, spinning your wheels again. Temptation might appear in the form of going out for a belt-busting family meal. Sunday mornings: do the kids want burgers, milkshakes and ice cream?

You can see by these examples that there are key areas where your willpower will be challenged – a crossroads if you like.

Do you break or do you stay committed when it comes to meeting your priorities?

The same principle applies for your professional life, your relationships and your personal development.

Are you committed to the decisions you have said you are going to make? Have you committed to the golden hour every morning? Have you committed to date night with your partner? Have you committed to reading a book on something that is relevant to helping you develop new skills and knowledge?

You have the opportunity when you stand at that crossroads to make the right decision or you could carry on being indecisive – or worse, make the wrong decision and continue to be frustrated and stressed.

While decisiveness is helpful, impulsiveness and impatience are most definitely not.

Have you made decisions on impulse, letting yourself get emotional and done something you regretted 24 hours later? I know I have. Sending an irate text message to someone or spiteful response to an email, for example.

There are many reasons people make poor and hasty decisions, and then regret them. Guilt and frustration tend to follow knee-jerk responses. You have to come up with a system that is going to help you take a second to think before you act.

You do it in other aspects of life. When the boss is going on at you, you don't thump him. (Well, I hope you don't!) You show restraint and you show patience.

Have you closed the front door as you get in after work and convinced yourself not to train at the gym tonight, without taking a second to think about whether or not that was the right thing to do?

If you did take a second, you would realise you do have time but you just can't be arsed!

You must add structure to your life. It allows you to think about your decision rather than just acting (or not!) on impulse.

Sometimes quick-thinking is required, but when it comes to you and your development and moving forward, consistent decisions that are made with thought behind them will help you win in the long game.

Avoid cutting corners with your decision-making and lifestyle planning to get the result you truly want as fast as possible.

DITCH THE BAD MOODS

How is your mood? How do you spend the majority of your day inside your own head? Are you happy or angry? Frustrated or stressed? Lost or in control? This will again take some honesty.

If you are unsure, why don't you ask your family or friends to be candid with you and ask them what they think? They will be truthful with you if you explain why you're asking.

To start with it may be quite hard to take, but it's important to face facts.

It can be cripplingly difficult as a man to express that you're feeling lost, frustrated and unfulfilled. How do you explain this to your mates down the pub?

Please don't be fooled into thinking you are the only person in this situation, just because it tends not to crop up in your banter with your mates. There are millions of men right where you are; struggling alone and suffocating in a life that has become more like a coffin.

Do you doubt your abilities? I do every day! Doubt is as regular as the sun coming up each morning. It is often the trigger for my low moods. It creates anxiety, stress and frustration.

Self-worth is a sensitive subject and one that is very hard to deal with.

Realising that you are important and that you do have a role to play is an important part of your growth. If you struggle with a lack of self-worth, do you hide it well from others?

TAKING GOOD THINGS IN LIFE FOR GRANTED

Another problem is having a blinkered view of life. When you feel your life is going down the pan, it's easy to focus on all the problems and obstacles that are stealing your lust for life.

This habit compounds your problems. It's like putting rose-tinted glasses on backwards, and everything you see is grey, gloomy and depressing.

The easiest way to resolve this is to always be grateful for the good things in life – no matter how small. A roof over your head. Food in the cupboard. A song on the radio that makes you smile.

Get into the habit of looking at the things that are going right to boost your mood.

BEING PESSIMISTIC ABOUT THE FUTURE

The future for a lot of men can be daunting. Self-doubt can hinder your aspirations to change to become the man you want to be. I've found that men who doubt themselves often hit hurdles when changing their life-style.

It can be hard to develop your mindset when you fail to have confidence in yourself. How can you learn to be positive about the future? What do you have to look forward to?

GOOD THINGS HAPPEN WHEN YOU CHALLENGE YOURSELF

One of my clients, Dave we'll call him, was 42 and had spent four years putting on weight because he was too afraid to go to the gym.

He was worried everyone would look at him. He didn't want to look stupid in front of others. His words! When I questioned why he would look stupid workout, he replied:

> *"I wasn't confident with using the machines and wasn't confident asking the instructor how to!"*

Anxiety crippled Dave's train of thought and held him back from achieving what he wanted to.

Fast-forward 14 months and Dave is now four stone lighter and is currently doing his level 2 gym instructor certification to help men who were in his position.

The moral of the story? Reach out to somebody who you think can help you achieve your goals. It's good for you and it's good for the person helping you.

Helping people achieve something that matters to them is a privilege in life. I was so honoured Dave contacted me and honoured to watch him grow over the year.

> Don't be afraid of what people think as it will hold you back from the life you want to lead. Put other people's thoughts out of your mind and commit to doing what you need to, to get the life you want.

LOW SELF-ESTEEM

I really hate to hear about guys having low self-esteem. Having a poor opinion of yourself means you have unrealistically low confidence in what you are capable of achieving.

Can you remember when it started? Has it always been this way?

Either way, try to remember a time when you walked with your head held high, when you had full confidence in yourself and everything that you did. Inside you were buzzing with ambition and drive. Form a picture of that time in your head. How do you remember it? How does it look?

So what is stopping you from being confident once again?

Our personalities are dictated by our own actions and mindset.

If you wanted, you could dress up real smart, scrub yourself up, look in the mirror and allow yourself to say

- *I will be positive today*
- *I will be confident today*

It's hard, really fucking hard. You first have to get yourself out of that coffin that you are in. Break the mould, get out of your comfort zone, and be brave and courageous.

There is a life waiting for you to live and it starts now!

FEELING ASHAMED OF WHERE YOU'VE GOT TO

You are where you are because of the decisions you've made. You have to come to terms with that and I understand that's not as easy as it might sound.

Over the years you may have let yourself go. It could be through:

- laziness
- poor planning
- poor self-awareness
- injury or illness
- a string of bad choices and excuses

You may look in the mirror and ask yourself how on earth you allowed yourself to get to the point you are at. You may feel ashamed by it.

Have you got to the point where going swimming with the kids is hard for you because you feel uncomfortable without a T-shirt on to cover up that flabby body of yours?

Use that energy, that emotion, anger and frustration with your situation, and use those feelings to fuel your focus in the coming months to turn your life around.

Have an "Eye of the Tiger" moment – stand up and fight for a better you.

A LACK OF IDENTITY

Between 2011 and 2015 I had no identity. When I left the Royal Marines I left behind my old persona, the sergeant, and closed that chapter of my life for ever.

It took me a long time to move on from that military identity where I had status and was an important figure. When I joined the civilian world, I didn't really have any identity or status, which led to self-doubt and low self-esteem. I felt really low. I was fighting to find out who I was, where I belonged and how I fitted into life. At that time, I just didn't know.

Of course, you don't need to have left the military after years of service to have an identity crisis as you get older.

A lot of men will go through life and ask themselves, 'What is my purpose?' And it's the lack of identity that causes frustrations in our mind. It plagues us with doubt about the future. It dampens the fire that burns in a man's stomach.

A good place to look for clues is to think about what you were like in your 20s, 30s and 40s.

TASK: REMEMBERING YOU

What you are doing

I want you to think back at other times in your life – in your 20s, 30s and 40s – and reflect on your situation and your hopes and dreams at those points. What got you excited about your life and where it was heading?

Why you are doing it

The ideas you had in the past may give you clues as to who you really are or what matters to you as a person.

This is helpful when you're feeling stuck and out of touch with what is important. It helps you reconnect with positive thoughts and feelings you have had in the past, and decide if you would like to feel that way again.

How to do it

I have put together a worksheet to help you do this. It's in the resources section and in the printed planner. Use this sheet to store your thoughts.

Think back to each decade of your life. Ask yourself what you thought you would be doing now.

Have you achieved what you wanted to and now need a fresh challenge in your life, or do you feel like you've not achieved enough? Could this be a reason you are lacking identity?

Without identity you are always going to struggle to move forwards. It doesn't happen overnight. It won't come easy. It will take some soul searching.

TOXIC RELATIONSHIPS

All your relationships will have some effect on you, whether they are positive or negative. It's important for you to understand how your relationships affect the things you do in life.

 Remember, your relationships range from those with a life partner to business partners, your children to team mates, your gym buddy to your friends and workmates. Have a think about all of them.

You will have a different type of relationship with everybody that you surround yourself with.

Life is so much easier when you surround yourself with positive relationships; ones in which you can truly be yourself. Isn't it a joy when you have others who support you in making your hopes and dreams come true?

Look at the people in your life with an open mind. Be honest. Are you happy in those relationships? Do you still want to be in them? Are you getting what you need from them to build you up? Or are you being dragged down?

I'm a firm believer that if you are not yourself around someone, if you pretend to be someone or something you're not, it's going to make things a lot harder for you. If you have not been happy in a relationship for a long time, it's time to cut loose.

Of course, people's personalities evolve over time so it is inevitable that the way other people think, act and see the world over time will change – that's something that you will have to accept. Growing apart is something that may end a relationship.

Business partners sometimes go their own way. Lifelong friends become distant. It's the same story for romantic couples too.

A good relationship is one that can adapt over time. It's strong because there is an acceptance of change and adjustments made to maintain that strong bond.

I have spoken to hundreds of men whose marriages are struggling because of their change in personality. If you are any in doubt as to whether it's you that has changed, ask the people closest to you - your parents, your spouse or your best friends.

Men quite often change as they near their 40s. It becomes harder to maintain fitness and mobility. A lot more aches and pains happen. Work commitments tend to take over life. The lack of structure and excitement can lead to frustration and stress.

Over the years, men seem to collect more pressures and responsibilities and, chances are, you are not the same person you were before you started to feel low and depressed.

When you feel like you're struggling, things can feel worse if the people closest are also the people who drag you down.

> *"You can't do that. You need to do this for me."*
> *"Forget the gym! Come and have a pint!"*
> *"Why are you going for that promotion? You're wasting your time!"*

Don't accept it.

You want people that encourage and support you in your life, not hold you back and make you question yourself.

TASK: CONDUCTING A DETAILED AUDIT

What you are doing

Now you know more about what can raise or lower your score, let's give your life a second audit.

Instead of the raw, gut instinct score you gave before, I want to your give some detailed reasons why you gave that rating.

Why you are doing it

Your initial gut reaction score is helpful – it provides a wake-up call, as well as a starting point for change.

But people tend to get the "finger in the air" scores a little out of whack compared to a more rigorous assessment of what's going on. You need to look at what's working and what's not in detail to get an accurate picture. Think of it as like making a pros and cons list.

Some people have a tendency to overestimate problems or deny them, while others become blind to their successes and only see failure. It's time to take stock of everything that's going on – good and bad. I'll tell you what we do with that information in the next chapter.

How you will do it

Have a look at the worked example in the resources section, then reflect on your own life for each of the four areas.

1. Download the audit sheet and print out four copies, one for each area of life, or use the planner
2. Choose an area to audit
3. Make a list of what is going well in the left column

4. Make a list of what is going wrong in the right column
5. Review both columns and see whether your overall score is accurate
6. Move onto the next area until all four are complete
7. Keep these audit forms safe as you'll be revisiting them for a task I've set in the next chapter

GETTING BACK ON TRACK

How do you feel after reading the last couple of chapters? Has the audit made you think more about your life and what's been holding you back? I hope that the "going right" things you jotted down in the last task help you see that there are still some things to be grateful for.

You might be feeling a bit despondent about your current circumstances and self-sabotaging behaviour. But fear not, because now I'm going to show you how to learn to reignite the fire in your belly to make those much needed changes to your life.

At the end of this chapter there is an exercise to start defining your perfect life, so you have something positive to focus on and work towards. It's a great way to start thinking creatively about how you would like life to be.

I'll also ask you to reflect on your detailed audit and identify the biggest difficulties you face, so you can consider the best way to prioritise beating them when you start putting your plan in place.

PAT YOURSELF ON THE BACK

If you have scored yourself and been honest, look in the mirror and pat yourself on the back. It's not easy to hold yourself up to scrutiny, especially when you first start out.

You have been truthful. You've made a note of how things are going and understood why some things are not going to plan. You also recognised what is working amid all the chaos. Now you can start an action plan for the future.

It's time to make the changes that are going to make you happy – changes to your life, your decision making, your mindset and your habits and routine.

Once you know who you are, what you want out of life and have started working towards it, then you are winning at life my friend.

But first a quick word of warning.

No matter how eager you are to transform your life, you must be cautious not to move too quickly too soon. Remember, with my system you have a year to get to your destination. You don't have to try to fix absolutely everything in a flash.

Going all out to implement a flawed plan is not a good idea. If you try to do a "big bang" change and fix everything overnight, it will cause more stress and frustration – exactly what you've said you want less of. Patience, grasshopper! You need a series of sensible stepping stones in the right places to cross the river... no blind running, jumping and hoping, yeah?

Focus your energy on creating a solid, workable plan. Concentrate on identifying a stretching but achievable objective for each of the four areas.

Recognising where you are right now in life is often grim. It can trigger emotions of despair and anger about how you let yourself get into this state.

Just accept that where you are right now isn't fun, but the journey to where you want to be will be. I promise. After all, I have walked many a mile in your shoes...

DIGGING DEEP ISN'T EASY

I once met a client for coffee and pretty much followed the process of the first chapter – learning about him, his situation, behaviours and surroundings.

I got him to write down paragraphs on each of the four life areas; how he felt, his struggles, etc. I didn't really have to say much as he focused on pouring all his thoughts out onto paper. The aim was to make him aware of how he had got to his position in life right then.

At the end I asked him to read back his notes. As he did he paused frequently and bit his lip in an attempt to hold in all the anger and frustration that had been hidden away.

When somebody is real with you and exposes your weaknesses, it's like getting a kick in the stomach – it is gut-wrenching and hurts. No wonder he needed those pauses to compose himself.

The good news is, once he knew where he'd come from and how he had got there, he could start making the steps to move forwards!

I could see it really takes some soul-searching and accountability to do what he did. That's why I want you to be proud of your honesty too.

Please don't beat yourself up if you feel disappointed with yourself! The pressures on men in their late 30s and 40s are big enough as it is!

Take comfort in the relief of getting all the things that frustrate or disappoint you down on paper and off your chest, especially if you have been carrying the burden of lying to yourself for a long time.

You know where you are and it is what it is. Now it is time for action.

IT'S TIME TO BE YOURSELF – TAKE OFF THE MASK

Unhappy people often wear masks. They wear one mask in front of their partner, another with their friends, and another at work. Do you present a different persona around different sets of people? I am guessing you do. It's a common problem.

The problem is, masks stop you – and others – from seeing the real you.

If you persist in hiding who you really are and what you are capable of, you will be unable to move forwards.

Low self-esteem, anger, frustration and depression will continue to dog your life and your sense of self-worth will diminish.

If you struggle with anxiety, depression or low self-esteem, do your friends know about it? I would guess not. These are things few men talk about with their friends. We should all open up a little more.

Make the effort to be more open about the way you feel and you will find that the majority of men are in the same situation as you. Surround yourself with positive people who appreciate you for who you are – people that you don't need to wear a mask to be around.

If you have been wearing a mask, then it can be pretty hard to get rid of it. It starts to feel like an old pair of slippers you just slide into.

It's tough to realise you've been doing it, to accept it and then to actually start being you again.

You need to be the real you to develop the habits, thinking, relationships and routine needed to get the life you want. Do that and the mask you have hidden behind will fall away naturally.

INCREDIBLE HULK AND DR DAVID BANNER

While I was trying to figure out who the hell 'I' was, I would end up getting so frustrated with trying to deal with the rest of the world.

I didn't thinking clearly. I made rash decisions. I coped badly with negativity or criticism.

I'd end up getting so angry I'd put my mask on and explode like the Hulk. I would push all those that were close to me away and never see reason.

It was very hard to come back from that; back to the person I really am and reveal the "David Banner" persona behind the mask.

When I was feeling human again, I regretted all the actions I had carried out as the Hulk.

You need to improve your coping mechanisms to be focused on the positives, improve your self-awareness of who you are, and the people you unintentionally hurt along the way.

Don't be the Hulk character stuck between two personalities. Get to grips with it. Take off whatever mask you put on to cope and be 100 per cent you.

Relationships are usually stronger and easier when you are honest. Being open when talking things over, like time, is an amazing healer.

The relationships you have are much easier without the mask getting in the way. If you are honest with your partner about your feelings and struggles then it will make your relationship stronger. Once you can show your true self to the people closest to you, you will feel comfortable enough to be open with your wider circle of friends too.

Take five minutes now to think about who is the real you? How does the real you act, feel and think before you apply the filter? It won't necessarily come right away.

Understand what your morals are, what your values and beliefs are, and what you stand for. Are you being held back somehow because you are not showing who you are?

Are you lying about the state of your health?

Are you continuing with relationships that are bringing you down?

Have a good, hard look at yourself, self-audit the mask and compare it to the real you.

Write the differences down and start identifying between the two. You can't keep wearing the mask and hiding your identity.

Show off who you really are and let everyone else accept it. Life is much less exhausting and much more rewarding that way.

GIVE YOURSELF PERMISSION TO TRY NEW THINGS

By getting rid of the mask, you also open the door to new opportunities. It's time to do some experimenting. It takes courage at first, but it gets easier.

Attending a new gym or fitness class can be an anxious experience.

It can be hard to turn up and ask for help. There is always the fear that you'll be last or not fit enough to finish a class.

So many guys are crippled by seeing their own reflection in the mirror and feeling ashamed about the way they look that it dulls their motivation to start.

But the new you – the real you – doesn't think like that. The real you allows you to overcome these fears because you know that it is going to benefit you in your life's goals. You know there are steps you must take to get like back on track.

By breaking down the barriers and overcoming fears, being who you should be, you can achieve your true potential – the very best version of you.

You can reignite the fire in your belly and set goals that you never thought possible. How many times have you said

I can't do that

How many times have you said

I'm going to do that

But you never did.

Start to understand that you can do it – and you must.

USE PLANS TO ADD MEANINGUL STRUCTURE TO YOUR LIFE

Looking back at your detailed audit, can you see what your priorities have been for the last six to 12 months? Have they been good choices or could they be improved? What needs to change in the coming year? What will you do more of? What will you do less of?

Planning and prioritising the things that happen in your life are crucial in this process. Spending a little time solving the causes of your problems will make all the difference.

(There is a whole chapter on creating your plan coming later in the book. For now I want to explain why planning matters and introduce some concepts to you.)

Your detailed life audit and regular weekly review sessions give you lots of examples of areas in which you could improve, and offer ideas about how you can break those problems down into simple, manageable steps to progress.

Let's take the problem of "no time to train" as it's a common issue for a lot of guys.

Look at your week from Sunday evening onwards and find the gaps you have to train. Can you hit the golden hour in the morning? Can you get 30 minutes in at lunch time? Could you walk or cycle to work even if just some of the way? Could you be more active by taking the stairs rather than the lift? Every little helps when you're starting out.

If your job prevents you from doing anything whatsoever, maybe look at the lifestyle choice. Is it really worth having a job that consumes your life completely? Yes you have bills to pay, but you weren't put on this planet purely to work and pay bills.

You only have one life and you're entitled to enjoy it. Perhaps your plan should be to get ready to jump ship.

WRITING THINGS DOWN BOOSTS COMMITMENT

One of the biggest steps that helped me to progress was just to write things down. It's so simple, yet invaluable.

Writing stuff down allows you to see the path in black and white. It holds you accountable. It helps you to become committed to your goals and the journey you will take. It acts as a constant reminder.

There is also a lot of neuroscientific research that proves writing things down helps them stick in your mind and boosts levels of success.

DECIDE WHAT NEEDS TO BE DONE AND DO IT

Most people will have used "to do" lists either at work, college or at home to stay focused. Planning what you want and what you need to do will make it easier to implement – be it hitting the gym, prepping your food, spending time with your family or completing a work task.

In your plan, you will prioritise these things as daily tasks that need to be followed through in order to live the lifestyle that you want. They should be non-negotiable.

When you wake up each day and review your schedule, get into the habit of ensuring these tasks are carried out.

Habit, routine and structure, repeat!

FOLLOWING YOUR PLAN CONSISTENTLY BUILDS GOOD HABITS

One of the hardest things to change when it comes to our journey thought life is habit. You have become so used to following bad habits that the process to change them to positive ones can be tricky at first.

Implementing a plan will help you to adjust to your new way of living. It allows you to set and commit to a manageable number of tasks and helps you stay focused and organised.

Without a plan of action, something to follow or guide you, the process of slipping back into those old ways is all too easy and those new habits you desperately need will never form.

By following your plan consistently you'll get to your destination in life. It's just like trusting your sat nav in the car to get where you need to be.

If you think back to your school days, you had a detailed timetable that mapped out everything you need to do during each school day, and you planned your time around that schedule.

You reviewed your timetable frequently and made sure you knew what you were doing, where and when. This helped to make sure things ran smoothly – you had your gym kit for PE and you'd done your homework for the next day's lessons.

And by doing that successfully and consistently you made progress, picked up some helpful habits, avoided getting told off, and made the most of each day.

IMPLEMENTING YOUR WEEKLY PLAN

The plan you will refer to most frequently from now on will be your weekly plan. This maps out the seven days ahead and the objectives for each day. It is the grown-up equivalent of your school timetable.

The purpose of following this plan is to be fully prepared for the day and week ahead, mentally and physically. There are no prizes for guessing that you are going to have a lot to deal with during the day, so it's vital that you get the body and mind ready to deal with whatever comes your way.

Build in time to focus on your plan twice a day – once in the morning and once in the evening. In between that, you will be doing what needs to be done in your plan.

I think of these as my morning and evening rituals, because they are something I do on autopilot without fail.

YOUR MORNING RITUAL

This determines whether your day is going to be successful or just one of those dismal days you chalk up to experience.

For some people, the idea of getting up a little earlier is met with a lot of resistance. To those people I say, "Just get on with it." Getting up early will solve a lot of big problems that make your life a struggle now.

As well as providing some breathing space and "you time", your morning ritual is a great time to look through your daily planner to see what has to happen for the day.

So many people think they know the plan in their head. Then once everything else that is going on in their life comes into play, things start to get muddled or lost. They end up losing focus by trying to remember what their plans or tasks were, instead of simply looking at it and taking action.

When you get busy, it's easy to forget what you have achieved and overlook what you should be doing.

Review your plan regularly throughout the day so that you stay on track. You can set up activity reminders to pop up on your smartphone at regular intervals to help you stay focused too.

That said; there are no distracting phones allowed during the morning ritual. No computers and no TV – just time for you. Sit and relax, workout, have breakfast, read a book, meditate, listen to music you love, take in a podcast, or enjoy the silence.

If you follow this protocol, then you will leave the house in a positive frame of mind. You will be all sorted for the day ahead. You will be more able to cope with any negativity or stress that comes your way because you are in a good frame of mind – not flustered and disorganised.

Following this morning routine also allows you to get used to being a little selfish with your time – after all, how much time do you get for yourself? It teaches you how to create boundaries and space in your life, so you can nurture yourself and improve your wellbeing.

You may love to help others and be there for everyone else, but you must learn to be a little selfish every now and then. Your time is precious, so make it count. Get your oxygen mask on first, remember?

If you don't make time to get your day off to a good start, remind yourself where it leads – to a build-up of stress, frustration and anger. These things snowball into poor habits like angry outbursts, over eating and excessive drinking.

A good way to escape reality in the morning is to read a fiction book. How good would it be to get engrossed in something that takes your mind away for a few minutes a day?

There are also Eastern practices that boost wellbeing, such as yoga or meditation. These have been shown to have a profound effect on mindset, and how you manage your thoughts and emotions. There are some great apps to help you meditate.

This time out is so important to your development, bettering your circumstances and getting the life you want and deserve. Make it a priority.

The breathing space provided by your morning ritual allows you to compose your mind, train your brain to filter all of the bullshit that goes on around you, the stresses that are bringing you down, and the environments that bring negative vibes.

You don't need that shit in your life. It's what made you feel lost and overwhelmed, right?

Commit to your morning ritual!

It's easy to stick to if you choose to do something fun and rewarding that you have been looking forward to.

YOUR END OF DAY RITUAL

Your routine at the end of the day is just as important as at the start. You need to focus on two things – what you need to do tomorrow (so you can be best prepared) and reviewing how today went.

Just like you review what's coming up in the morning, you can also review your plan for the next day in the evening.

How about packing the things you need for tomorrow the night before?

Prepare the food and snacks you want to eat to avoid the stress that comes with rushing at the last minute before you have to leave the house. It's also a good idea to look a few days ahead into your plan too. Like a good boy scout, *be prepared.*

As well as thinking about what you need to do, the other thing to ponder on is how the day went. This will make a big difference to your habits, routines and overall structure of your life. The process won't take long once you get into the swing of it and you'll find you do it on autopilot over time.

Don't worry if you miss the occasional item – focus on what you are achieving and what you can do better next time.

Another excellent mindset technique to add into your evening ritual is to look for things to be grateful for. (You'll remember I told you if you don't make time to notice the good things in life, you are more likely to feel down.)

It's so important to harness the power of gratitude. Even on the darkest of days, there is *always* something to be grateful for – a roof over your head, a smile from a kind stranger, your car starting first time, someone letting you out at a busy junction, singing along to a great song on the radio, a joke that made you smile, food on the table, or a pet that runs to greet you when you get home.

I want you to get into the habit of writing down a list of good things that happen to you each day – however small. It trains your brain to be more positive and boosts happiness.

Keep reminding yourself with gratitude statements each day so you take enjoyment from the little things in life again.

Your statements will quickly build into a big list of reminders of just how lucky you actually are.

Reviewing the all the things you can be grateful for – especially when you're feeling fed up – will lift your spirits. It can also be a prompt to do something you enjoyed again.

Try to come up with three things every day that you are grateful for, but list more if you want to.

By writing things down you have a visual reminder and mental reinforcement. It helps you create a positive mindset that will make you much more resilient when life inevitably throws a curve ball.

Another thing that some men find helpful is journaling. This technique can also fit in well with your end of day ritual.

Journaling simply means writing your thoughts down. They don't have to make too much sense. You don't have to share your words with anyone else. The purpose is simply to break free from having everything going on in your head – to get it all out onto paper, and to stop it taking up brain power that could be better used. Read it back later if you want.

When guys review their journal entries; it often helps them gain a better understanding of their thoughts and feelings. They are free from the stressful situation they perhaps found themselves in at the time of writing, and can gain important insights to help them make better choices in future.

You don't want to come home and take things out on the people you care about most. Equally, it can be hard to speak out because of the fear it could be misinterpreted, accidentally hurts someone's feelings or worries them – which means you end up bottling things up.

If your worries sit with you then you are likely to drink through it to feel better, be snappy with the people that matter or generally make bad decisions. Not good.

Spending time focusing on your gratitude statements or venting in your journal are much better options in the long term.

REFLECT ON HOW WOULD YOU LIKE YOUR LIFE TO BE

Another useful technique for getting life back on track is to think about what life would be like if you had no obligations or restrictions placed upon you. This is called designing your perfect day. Let's have a look at how it works.

TASK: WHAT WOULD YOUR PERFECT LIFE LOOK LIKE

What you are doing

It's time to go into your imagination. Forget where you are right now and get dreamy about what a day in your perfect life would be like. As a kid, did you want every day to be as exciting as Christmas? Have you ever spent time wondering what would you like to happen now you're a grown man? It's time to get your thinking cap on.

Why you are doing it

By imagining days in your perfect life, you give yourself permission to think about the good things you want to happen. You can free yourself from the short and medium-term problems you face and come up with ideas about what you want to do to feel more fulfilled.

How you do it

Have a think about these big questions to get started and then think about your responses so you can start to plan what needs to happen to live your perfect lifestyle.

- If money was no object, what would you do?
- What do you love to do most?
- What new knowledge and skills will you have mastered?
- What will be giving you comfort and security?
- What will give your challenge and excitement?
- Who would you most like to do these things with?
- Where would you be living?
- Who will you be spending your life with?

TIP: You'll also get some ideas from the "Remembering your past" task– those hopes and dreams in your 20s, 30s and 40s that I asked you to jot down.

Have a think about how you can start incorporating these into your life.

Some of the things you add will be quick and relatively easy to achieve, like spending more time with your loved ones. Becoming a world-famous astronaut like Tim Peake might take a little longer ☺. Be on the lookout for quick wins – things that you could start doing easily.

And remember, your bigger dreams can be broken down into those simple, manageable stepping stones to get you to where you need to be.

If you can't afford your dream car just yet, maybe you can have a track day in one? Prioritise these things that make your heart flutter with excitement once more.

LEAVE YOUR OLD LIFE BEHIND

You probably have a lot to think about right now. It's a lot to take in, but the good news is this new information is what's going to help you break free from the prison that your current life has become.

Your detailed audit scores have opened your eyes to the way you are living your life at the moment and have shown the good and bad things happening.

The perfect life task has shown you the way you could be living if you had more structure and better habits.

The next step for you is trying to make sense of it all and make your plan to move forwards.

IDENTIFY YOUR PRIORITIES

The self-audit built up a picture of exactly what is going on in your life – good and bad.

You can clearly see which areas are weakest in your life because they have the most or the biggest problems. These are the things that take you furthest away from your perfect day. Perhaps those need attention first. One of the biggest problems people encounter is the overwhelming temptation to change everything at once.

Yes, you really want to sweep your problems away now you've seen the power of planning, but acting hastily often means oversights and unintended consequences.

Have you ever dashed off to the supermarket to grab the ingredients for dinner, only to unpack your shopping at home and realise you forgot something vital? As the proverb says, *"Act in haste, repent at leisure."*

Trying to tackle all the issues you have all at the same time will put a lot of pressure on you. It's OK to take one step at a time.

Remember, your progress should be like stepping stones, moving from one well-defined point to another, not having a run at it and trying to cross the river in one big bold leap. Be kind to yourself. And realistic!

TASK: WHAT'S THE BIGGEST PROBLEM

What you are doing

I want to you spend some time looking at your four areas of life and the detailed audit scores you gave. Then have a look at your perfect day and look at how you would prefer life to be.

These will give you clues about how to start making changes that will boost your wellbeing.

Why you are doing it

Your resources are not limitless and you need to prioritise to avoid over-whelm. There are only so many hours in a day. Your bank balance has a finite limit. You have to work out the most efficient way to bring about the biggest changes that will genuinely be achievable.

You also need to make sure you are being realistic – no more "New Year's Resolution" syndrome, where you get too ambitious and your good intentions quickly fizzle out to nothing.

You need to choose what elements on the "cons" list you are going to address.

How you are doing it

Before you start your assessment, have a look at my worked example. in the resources section.

1. Review your self-audit for each of the four areas and next to each item jot down a score for each of the following criteria

   1.1. problem severity – does it ruin lots of aspects of your life

   1.2. the frustration it causes – how much it takes you away from your perfect day

   1.3. quick wins you could put in place to make rapid improvements

2. Identify the biggest problem(s) for each of the four areas and simple changes you can make or steps you can take to be free of them

3. Decide what you need to do to make that happen

4. Make a promise to yourself you will solve these problems

5. Keep your worksheets safe, you'll need them when start developing your plan

HOW TO CREATE YOUR PLAN TO MOVE FORWARDS

Now you know what needs to change in your life and why you finally want to be free of those struggles, it's time to put a plan together to make sure it happens.

Your plan is broken down into manageable chunks and put into a yearly, 12-week, weekly and daily timetable. You will be structuring your daily routine and actions towards making consistent progress until you reach your yearly goal.

Before we look at planning, I want to address something that often stops people before they start. Let me prove to you that you can fit in these new things and still get the boring "adulting" stuff done too.

HOW TO DO WHAT YOU WANT AND STILL MEET YOUR OBLIGATIONS

Much as you might dream about it, you and I know, you can't abandon everything in life that you don't want to do.

If you go on strike and stop washing up, after two days you're out of pans and dishes and end up having to do the washing up. Yes, you can stop doing some things in life you're not fond of, but not everything. There has to be some "adulting" going on to balance things up – you can't escape it.

The trick is to make time for your life-enhancing priorities alongside your core commitments, rather than let every potential commitment that crops up steal the time you have at your disposal to do things that matter to you!

 Remember Parkinson's Law – "work expands to fit the time available..." You have to protect your "you time" ruthlessly otherwise it will vanish!

The simplest way to fit in your new activities is to break your objectives up into lots of small steps that will fit into your day. With patience and consistency, you will see big results over the long term. Just like a marathon is run one step at a time.

Let's look at an example.

Imagine you have decided to start prioritise health. You want to lose a stone and a half. How can you meet that priority in the 12-weeks you have available?

You would start off by listing the one-off tasks you need to do up front, maybe

- research local gyms
- join the gym that suits you best
- hire a personal trainer
- sort out an exercise and nutrition plan
- buy a FitBit, install a smartphone app or get a simple pen and paper to track your activity levels

Those will be quick to cross off your to do list – a few hours work at most. That can be fitted in by ditching some telly time, getting up a bit earlier or using your lunch hour. Easy.

Then there will be the ongoing tasks that will depend on the resources – time and money – you have available. This is where you might need to juggle things around to get everything to fit.

If you're short on time then three gym sessions a week rather than five will be more realistic and sustainable in the long term. If you've got the cash, you could have your trainer with you at each session to keep you accountable. But if money is tight, group bootcamp sessions will be cheaper and your new fitness friends will help you stick with it.

If you can't get the plan to work because your goal is too ambitious, use a longer time frame rather than abandon it. If you can only do two gym sessions a week and the fitness programme you chose says you need five to succeed, then something's got to give.

In this case give yourself two milestones. Commit to losing a stone in the first 12 weeks and the remaining half a stone in the next 12. The world won't end if you take a little bit longer. You are taking those steps in the right direction. The main thing is you're making yourself a priority and getting back in shape, rather than flouncing off and making excuses about why you can't do it, right?

The planning process might feel like spinning a lot of plates on a lot of poles to start with but it gets easier.

Have a look at the worked examples I've given to help you find your feet with the process. (I have specifically chosen the most common things my clients want to plan, so you will find some useful tips.)

On the topic of tips, this next one – the CICR effect – is really powerful.

THE CICR EFFECT

CICR is something I'm religious about. It works well for me and hundreds of my clients. It really helps you stick to your plan and not let too many obligations take over your life again. I don't want you slipping back into your old ways.

It's a really simple system to remember and apply.

CICR stands for

- **Commitment**
- **Implementation**
- **Consistency**
- **Review**

Commitment brings success because you are dedicating yourself to a cause, in this case, your life. If you can learn to commit to your plan to improve your life in the areas that you struggle in, and you know what you want to achieve, you will become a success.

Implementation means actually doing it! So many people go wrong because they talk a good game but never follow through. It's about starting. Once you do, with your commitment, there should be no looking back. Or stopping.

Consistency means continuously moving forwards with your journey. Little steps every day moving you ever closer to the point you want to get to. Just like the stepping stones across the river, rather than taking a run at it!

Review means checking your actions against your goal. You need to make sure what you're doing is actually making a difference and that you are doing it. Reviewing stops you from slipping or becoming complacent with your objectives.

Let's have a look at how CICR might work with weight loss.

You need to have that line in the sand moment, the epiphany when you grab your beer belly and decide it's finally time to make a change. Use your "why" to motivate you. You must *commit* to changing your lifestyle.

You need to have a manageable workout programme and a meal plan to *implement*. You need to do something different because your old ways were not working. Implementing a proven system makes a lot of sense.

You need to stick to your good habits – doing regular exercise, eating right, and swapping ale for water *consistently* to lose weight. The more inconsistent you are, the slower your progress. If you abandon your good habits, you make no progress or worse still, start regressing.

You need to *review* your programme and how closely you are following it.

You need to log your workout sessions to see if you're getting fitter and stronger. You need to measure your food to make sure you're not over-eating. You need to dig out your tape measure and check your stats. You need to stand on the scales. You need to see how snug your jeans waistband is.

You can see here, if one part of CICR is missing, so are your chances of success!

WHAT IS IN A GOOD PLAN

For a plan to work it needs to be balanced. Although you can't fix everything in one go, you can make progress in all four areas at once. All you do is vary they amount of progress you need to make to match your priorities for each area, so the most important one is met first.

Here's a reminder of those four areas

- personal development
- health
- work or business
- relationships

Some coaches say you should just target one area. I disagree. If one area is weak – relationships for example – then it's likely to mean that other areas of life are going to suffer.

Drinking in the pub to avoid a looming argument at home may also lead to grabbing an extra-large kebab on the way back and a screaming hangover the next day. You skip your morning ritual and workout for a lie-in. You don't make any healthy food because you can't face eating anything. Because you feel ill, the time at work drags. Someone snaps at you for making a mistake. You get home in a bad mood, full of frustration and anger – which leads to more arguments.

 Remember, poor choices in one area tend to snowball and they can spill over into other aspects of your life.

Put together a plan that is going to make it easy to make lots of good choices and speed up your progress in attaining the more of the *perfect day* life you want.

Some goals might go well together, others might not.

For example: if you want to have a lot of exciting city breaks with your partner, it's going to be harder to stick to your healthy eating plan if you are tempted to dine out. Perhaps going on weekend breaks where you can go for long walks in the hills during the day, would be a better choice. You still spend time together, but without derailing your fitness goals.

MAKE YOUR PLAN WATERTIGHT

Planning may take you some time to start with. The structure may seem cumbersome and you might wonder if what you are doing is right.

The best thing is to make a start and then refine it.

You can mentally rehearse going from one step to another and make sure your strategy is broadly sound. Just like weather forecasters can get caught out by something unexpected, you can't plan for every single eventuality. However, you can cater for most of them well in advance.

A solid plan, one that isn't rushed and is well thought-out, will be a benefit to your life in the long run. If you were able to plan your week each day and by the hour, you will be in complete control of your life. It might sound restrictive, but you are filling your life with things that boost your wellbeing physically and mentally – and that is actually very freeing.

Since birth you have become better at most things you do – writing, reading, talking etc. Like any new skill, by doing something over and over again in life will mean you improve at it and it's the same with planning.

It doesn't matter how long it takes you to complete this first plan. Give or take a day or two, maybe a week tops. That's fine.

A good strategy is to do your first draft plan on Saturday, sleep on it, and then refine it on Sunday. That's enough time for big mistakes in your assumptions to spring to mind and for you to deal with them, before you begin implementing your plan in more detail.

Don't use the excuse that you need to make umpteen revisions to your plan to make it bombproof before you can start following it though. That's not true. It's more important to gain experience in developing your planning skills and working towards a better life for you.

For now, focus on putting together something that's going to solve those big problems that have been getting you down without labouring over it and see how it goes.

THE IMPORTANCE OF VARIED DEADLINES

By using plans with different deadlines, you can look further ahead. You need to get away from short-term thinking. It's unrealistic for a lot of changes you'll need to make. Giving yourself a longer time frame takes a lot of pressure off and still gets the job done (thanks to the CICR effect).

What's your plan for the next 12 months?

How about the next five years?

Your plans don't have to be as detailed for longer time-frames. The detail is in your weekly and daily schedule. Just make sure that all your stepping stones added up will get those big results you're after.

Another benefit to completing the yearly plan is that you learn to become patient. A year is a long time to stick with your objectives. If it feels like an eternity, remember how much worse not planning feels. How many times have you watched a year go by and find yourself still stuck at square one, wishing you had started the process 12 months ago!

Longer-term goals force you to think bigger. Why? Because you have more time to accomplish more. Unlike your daily and weekly plans, the long-term plans stop you from playing small with your hopes and dreams.

Think about someone who wants to run a marathon. Expecting to run 26.2 miles this Tuesday with no training is daft. Expecting to run one in six months after consistently following a training plan is definitely doable. The longer time-frame helps you achieve some magical things with your life.

HOW TO SIZE UP AND BALANCE YOUR PLAN

When you plan for a year you have to be bold with your goals. Don't overwhelm yourself, but also don't sell yourself short. With a year to work on your priorities, you can achieve a lot.

Dream big!

If you've got a moment right now, have a look at your perfect day notes. Which of those are achievable in the next 12 months?

When selecting your yearly goals for each area, decide what matters most to you. Why? Because the more meaningful the goal, the easier it is to stay motivated, get out of bed in the morning with a bounce and follow the process.

To give you some ideas about how to approach it, here are some suggestions for common goals my clients have for each area.

PERSONAL DEVELOPMENT YEARLY GOALS

Personal development goals add more strings to your bow when it comes to achieving your other life targets.

For your yearly goals in this area, I recommend you focus on adding balance and breathing space to your life, and then look at the skills you need to develop to help you achieve success in other areas.

Look for books you can read, courses you can take and exercises you can do that give you the inner resources you will need to succeed.

EXAMPLES

Commit to the golden hour each morning

Your golden hour, if implemented consistently, will allow you to find enough time to focus on your own personal development, whether that's time working out, reading, listening to a podcast or doing yoga.

The 60 minutes you set aside for yourself should have a purpose and include several activities. Decide what you will do to make the rest of the day or week run more smoothly.

Also include things that are fun, like strolling to the park to enjoy the sunrise. Don't wait to decide what you are going to do on the morning you do it – it wastes time. You need to be doing, not thinking about doing. This is a great goal to set because it makes achieving all your goals easier.

Learn new skills for improving your health, wellbeing and success

Personal development is learning to set and implement plans to meet goals. The more you know about goal-setting, motivation, resilience and focus, the better. Need some cooking skills and recipe ideas to meet your healthy eating goals? Work out what you need to learn.

TIP: Have a look at the recommended reading section for some good ideas about what to choose for your golden hour.

HEALTH YEARLY GOALS

Fitness is an incredible medicine for those who suffer with low confidence and self-esteem. In my darkest hours I turned to fitness to get me through each day.

Having a good sweat by pushing yourself in the gym or at class releases endorphins, which are hormones that make you feel amazing. Improving your fitness is a great way to handle frustration and stress. If you've had a bad day at the office then go and take it out on a spin bike or in the weights room. Even a brisk walk in the fresh air can work wonders. How about committing to 10,000 steps a day?

Any time you are tempted not to set a big health goal, remind yourself that you want to be here for another 60 years to watch your children grow up or enjoy later life. So many people neglect themselves without realising our bodies are our biggest asset and should be the main focus in our lives.

Mobility and flexibility can become a real issue as we get older. Can you still touch your toes? Can you sit cross-legged? You often neglect these important elements of your life. Life gets a lot harder the less you can move. You must include mobility in your lifestyle; perhaps add stretching to your golden hour.

The fitter you are and the better your diet is, the more energy you are going to have. The more energy you have, the more you can get done.

EXAMPLES

I will commit to running around the park with my children on Saturdays

Playing with the kids is a real and emotional example of ensuring your health is in tip-top form. Are you too tired to have a kick-about of the football with the children? Are you out of breath running 10 yards for a Frisbee?

This can be embarrassing, infuriating and upsetting. Commit to changing that.

Sign up for a 5K run

You probably aren't up for a marathon, but you could do a 5k event, right? By having a specific event to train for, you will be focussed in your training sessions.

I signed up to a 100 mile run, which I completed on the 10th June. Before signing up for this I was unfocused during training sessions as I lacked direction.

The 4 month process of preparing myself for this event allowed me to focus on my one key goal, it also helped me focus on other aspects of my life such as business, family etc.

Lose four stone in weight

Everyone knows the health benefits of losing excess body fat. Remember this is a yearly goal, so you have 12 months to work on it. Think about your ideal weight and what you have to achieve on a weekly or monthly basis to meet that target. Go for something realistic in the longer term, like one pound of fat a week. Then add that up to be your annual goal.

TIP: I have shared a lot of short, effective workouts on my YouTube channel. You don't need any equipment or a gym, just a bit of free space to move about is all that's required. Find out more here: www.youtube.com/channel/UC2pK0k7xyutObbpd6UPPV7A

Eat healthily 90 per cent of the time

When it comes to nutrition, try to keep to a 90/10 per cent split on clean eating. That means you spend 90 per cent of the week getting it right and for the remaining 10 per cent you reward yourself for your efforts – your favourite indulgent food or a couple of beers.

I do not advise going for 100 per cent as a target because it is too restrictive. The 10 per cent of treats won't derail your efforts but will significantly boost your chances of sticking with it in the long term.

Cut down on alcohol

Alcohol acts like a self-destruction for the majority of men. You get home annoyed or fed up and the next thing you know you are six beers down to numb the pain, thinking that everything is going to be OK. But then the hangover ruins the next day. Commit to cutting down on your intake and find other ways to manage stress and relax.

You might have thought it's a *quick fix* but it's a *bad one that actually doesn't fix anything.* Control your intake, and ensure that you don't abuse booze if you are going to focus on your health. Think about setting a limit and committing to writing down how much you do have – it's easy to lose track.

PROFESSIONAL LIFE YEARLY GOALS

There is nothing worse than not being motivated to turn up to work. My son always tells me he hates going into school. I tell him: "Son, if you go to school and do well you will be able to get a good job, earn plenty of money and you can then buy every wrestler on eBay..."

It does the job every time!

What motivates you? Set goals that will motivate you to enjoy your professional lifestyle.

Becoming more motivated and giving yourself purpose will help you start to grow. You will get better at what you do and have pride behind your actions.

What do you want out of your job? What needs to happen for you to be happy, successful and away on time to be home for the family meal?

I appreciate it can seem impossible to change your career if you feel you need to, but you've got a year to make the changes.

Be bold!

EXAMPLES

Work towards a professional certification

It's great to have something to aim for in your professional life; something that is going to make you proud of all the hard work you've put in.

Working towards a certification is a great example. It helps with your personal development, your growth, your reputation and gives you focus. These are all positive things that will help you move forwards.

It can also be a great way to change career altogether. The certification proves that even though you might be the new kid on the block, you are skilled in that area.

Get a promotion

What do you need to do in order to get a promotion? What is your boss or organisation looking for? Maybe you need to move to a new company to progress?

Have a think about what needs to happen to make you more fulfilled in your work life.

Add a new product or service range to my business

Why not offer something new in your business? It's a great opportunity to add some variety to your day-to-day work and it will stretch you.

I decided to set a goal to write this book so I could help more guys get their life on track. I'd never written a book before, so it made an excellent yearly goal.

RELATIONSHIPS

Good relationships make life enjoyable. Arguing is not fun.

Doing thoughtful or considerate things for people who matter to you feels good. Once you've got your oxygen mask on, go right ahead and help others. This goes without saying.

If you let someone out from the junction when you're out driving, you feel pretty good, right? The other person says thank you with a wave and you drive off pleased with yourself, just with a random act of kindness for a stranger.

Now imagine what cheering up friend who's not coping well by taking them out for a nice meal or buying a gift for your partner could do. These small gestures over time go a long way to building strong and supportive relationships. Make time to do this.

The more strong relationships you build, the bigger your support network will grow. This could be friends, family, business associates or team mates.

Setting relationship goals will reinforce how much the people you hold closest matter to you – partners, children or parents. For most people, these relationships are their "why".

It's very easy to take those closest to you in this world for granted. You look at your busy schedule and usually the sacrifice comes in the way of quality time with your nearest and dearest. You now have an opportunity to change that.

EXAMPLES

Get up earlier to spend more time with family in the evening

This is a simple concept and links up nicely with the golden hour. Mornings can be really hectic. However, if you get your day off to a good start, you arrive at work feeling in control and ready to make a start.

When you're organised, it's easier to stay focused on one topic at a time, which boosts your productivity. Being more productive means you don't have to stay late to try to get things done. This means you can get home early to spend time with the family and put the kids to bed.

This routine takes practice, but it is definitely worth it.

Join five-a-side football team rather than go to the pub

Swapping a heavy session down the pub for five-a-side football is a great way to keep you off the booze while still socialising.

You get to meet new people, widen your circle of friends, boost your fitness and cut down your alcohol intake. If you didn't believe in "quadruple whammies" before, you should do now.

Do some work for charity

If you want to improve your self-worth and make a difference in other people's lives and your community, then charity work is a great option. This is a rewarding way for you to do some good in the world and will help boost your self-esteem.

Plus helping people in a worse situation than you is a great way to feel grateful for the good things in your life and not take them for granted.

Have date night once a week

Do you have a regular date night with your partner? This doesn't have to be an expensive thing. It doesn't have to be a meal out with drinks. Maybe choose a film to watch at home? Why not just turn your phones off and see how each other is doing over a cup of tea. This can make a real difference to a relationship that matters.

Again – set a night that works for both of you and make it part of your weekly routine. Make sure it doesn't clash with your five-a-side football plans, your hour spent brushing up your French lingo for your up and coming holiday or whatever else it is you decided your other goals might be.

Set aside Sundays for being with the children

For me, weekends are for nothing else other than the kids and family. A whole day with together, uninterrupted.

Never undervalue the need for quality time with your children. They deserve to have fun and share some great experiences with their dad, yes? They should not be stuck with someone who is distracted and dreading the week area.

TASK: ANALYSING WHAT NEEDS TO CHANGE

I want you to review and assess the detailed self-audit task you did earlier.

Start thinking about the four areas and brainstorm some ways to make improvements. Have a look at each idea and think about what achieving each one could mean to you.

You don't want to rush this part; it has to be right. Have a look at my worked example in the resources section to give you some pointers.

STEP 1: REVIEW WHAT'S WORKING

Before you start planning improvements in your life, take some time to review what is working for you right now. For each of the four headings, look at what's going well and why. It's good to be reminded about what's not gone totally pear-shaped. Plus, you can plan what you want to improve further or do more of.

STEP 2: REVIEW WHAT'S FAILING / FAILED

Now look at the areas that need the most development. Follow the same process and review your detailed self-audit. Under each of the four headings, list the areas you feel you need most development and write why you think it is failing.

You may know the answer, but if will certainly help to review these issues and get you thinking. Look at the ones you want to focus on.

STEP 3: BRAIN DUMP POSSIBLE SOLUTIONS

Take the list of areas you need to develop and start thinking about possible solutions.

This process of putting pen to paper gets everything that you are thinking out of your head and becomes something you can view and review.

Don't hold out for the perfect solution, think of all the different ways that you can address those issues and create a better way of living for yourself.

When you start to write down possible solutions to your problems, you pop your creativity hat on – this is your chance to try some new strategies and have fun with the process.

Pick out quick wins – some issues that can be solved really quickly. For example if you've decided date night needs to be a thing, simply pick the most convenient time. These quick wins help you realise you are in control of your life and can make progress and feel much happier very quickly indeed.

Of course, not all the problems you need to solve will be quick wins – but make the most of the ones you can.

For the longer term goals, you'll need to plan the time you will need to make consistent progress and what you will be doing.

Sometimes you will need to do the same thing each time, for example preparing healthy meals for lunches at work will broadly stay the same in terms of skills and effort. Some goals will mean a change in pace over time, such as if you want to become fluent in a new language, you will progress from the beginners to intermediate to advanced level, and not stay at the beginners level for the whole 12 months.

HOW TO PLAN

Now you have an idea about the sort of things you want to include in the plan, let's have a look at how to put a plan together.

After I've explained the process, I want you to put your plan together by completing the guided tasks that follow.

HOW TO PLAN A YEAR

You are looking for the best solution across the four areas of your life so you gain momentum over the coming 12 months.

You have brainstormed a list of all the ways you could meet your goals. You have a lot of options to move forward.

Have a reread of your ideas and think about

- which ones excite you most
- which ones have the most powerful "whys"
- which seem the most feasible
- which will make you happiest
- which will make you the least frustrated
- which ones go well together
- which ones clash

What combination of those goals and options are going to get you the best result?

Remember to dream big!

Once you have your yearly goals set, it's time to start looking at the next level of detail in the 12-week plan.

HOW TO PLAN FOR 12 WEEKS

This process allows you to make realistic targets to attain in 12 weeks. The progress you make in each of the quarters will contribute to achieving the final year goals.

This is where the magic happens. Everything starts to seem much more *doable*, which is very exciting and motivating. You can see there really is light at the end of the tunnel (and it's not someone with a torch coming along to give you more work!).

You need to make sure that each 12-week goal, when put together, will create the big result you want.

As you've not got much planning experience at this stage, let's have a look at some good ways to go about it.

The easiest way is to review your brain-stormed list of solutions and see which ones will suit each 12-week block best.

What order do you need to do them in?

Another approach is to imagine you have the result already, and reverse engineer the steps you need to take to get there.

Consider the final step you would need to take before you got the end result and then ask what you would need to do immediately before that. Repeat that process until you end up at your starting point. Now run through the steps in the correct order and check the process works. If a step is missing or needs changing, make some changes and then run through again.

You can, of course, just run through from the start to the finish. This is handy if you don't have much experience with reaching that sort of goal.

Let's look at an example – a weight loss scenario for getting rid of middle-age spread that has snuck up on someone.

Imagine you wanted to lose two stone in a year. What might your first key step be?

If you didn't know anything about fitness and nutrition, the first thing you would probably do is hire help – a personal trainer to help with exercise and food advice.

Once you've hired the person, the trainer would put together a fitness programme to suit your lifestyle. You would assess if a home-based workout or gym sessions be most appropriate. How many times a week could you train? Would you go on a cookery course to learn how to make healthy food? Maybe you would buy some recipe books? Or use a plan that the trainer provides.

You would continue this process, working through each step in turn until you get to the end result you want for the end of the year.

Then you would divide those steps up into your 12-week blocks.

You don't need to go into lots of detail about how you will achieve each of the steps at this stage. That comes later. Just make sure you have a complete list of the major milestones and that they are manageable in a 12 week period.

 Be patient and thorough. If you rush the planning, you're likely to make mistakes. Your plan must be feasible. The last thing you want to do is send yourself down another a blind alley because you didn't thoroughly check where you were going before you headed off.

Cutting corners means you will come unstuck later when you hit unforeseen problems.

Remember the analogy of crossing the river. You have to cross by taking the stepping stones rather than having a good run up, jumping into the air and expecting to reach the other side in one go. Rushing, though understandably tempting, is an unhelpful strategy that is doomed from the start.

If you do want to make rapid progress with much less risk attached, have a look at how other people have achieved something similar. Perhaps they have written a book about their experience or have a blog that shares their stepping stones in detail? This research would be a good way to cut down on your planning time, learn more about how to achieve the result, and get some handy hints, tips and insights.

Another tip is finding out who can follow you on your journey? When you look at your plan, consider which things you can do with others. This will often help you meet your relationship goals and can also help with holding yourself accountable.

Will you work out with like-minded people? What relationships will you build along the way? Maybe you will join that five-a-side football team and make some new friends. Have you thought about including your partner along for the bike rides you want to do? It may bring your relationship closer.

Once you have the targets sorted out, it's time to map out the first 12 weeks out in detail, which you'll do with weekly plans.

Do this weekly planning one quarter at a time as you may need to make adjustments along the way if your progress is faster than you imagined.

Equally, sometimes you get a massive, unexpected curveball in life and you'll need to adjust your plans accordingly.

It's not a good use of time to try to note down a whole year's worth of weekly plans. Have an idea in your mind's eye and firm it up nearer the time.

HOW TO PLAN A WEEK

This is where you start to get a really good idea of the stepping stones you're going to use to hit your 12-week target.

You can see exactly how you're going to make progress and free your mind of clutter. The constant internal dialogue in your brain can be overwhelming and drag you down into a pit of stress and frustration.

This mental "space" makes life much easier to deal with, boosts your mood, makes achieving your targets easier and raises your level of success.

Once you clear your mind by getting the details for the week down on paper you are able to think a lot more clearly going forward. You cannot help but be more focused, because your mind isn't flitting from one random thought to the next trying to decide what's best. You know what's best, because you planned it that way.

It's not by accident that the most unfocused people of all are those who fail to plan, because they drift from problem to problem, shiny thing to shiny thing, and are always reactive rather than proactive. It leaves them wondering why they feel at the mercy of everything and in control of nothing.

By noting everything important you need to do in a given week – your gym sessions, Frisbee with the kids in the park, date night, working on your new website – you can be sure you will get it done. No more clashes and double bookings. No more lurching unprepared from one task to the next.

There is another important job that your weekly plans do for you. They help you to manage and measure progress.

This is where the rubber hits the road. As well as guiding you and helping you organise your activities in the most efficient way, your weekly plans let you measure your progress in detail.

How can you possibly know where you are in your progress if you don't track it? It's so much easier to find yourself drifting in life if you don't pay attention to where you're heading.

Did you really read for 30 minutes every day over the past week, or did you miss a couple of sessions? If you tick it off in your list, you know for sure.

 Remember the R in the CICR formula. You need to review your progress to make sure you stay on track and put contingency plans in place if needed.

As with 12-week goals, this weekly time-frame allows you to prioritise and create a sequence. It provides an efficient order to your actions so you get results quickly.

As well as reviewing as the week unfolds, you can also imagine how things will pan out in the future.

For example, are you planning to go on a two-week, all-inclusive holiday this quarter and will have no gym time then? Your weight loss goal doesn't go well with all-you-can-eat holidays so how can you stay on track? You'll need a strategy, so what will it be?

Are you going to fit in a few extra workouts before and after you go? Maybe you could do something active while you're away like those wind-surfing lessons you always wanted or hiking to see the mountain views?

Are you going to skip the three-course lunch and just have the main course?

If you know in advance then you can adjust and fine-tune your approach, so you can still enjoy yourself without letting bad habits and apathy creep in when you come back home.

Weekly plans can also help you stay on top of important activities and events that are on the horizon. These are things that often matter a lot to other people such as birthdays, anniversaries, and other celebrations. Your weekly planning will keep you on top of this.

Once you have your list of things to do for the week, you can start thinking about your plans for each day. These two plans are closely related. You might have to juggle what's in both to get it to run smoothly and meet your objectives. I'll explain how to do that shortly with the Sunday brain dump strategy.

HOW TO PLAN A DAY

Avoid the temptation to dwell on how big and far away your yearly goals may seem. It's very unhelpful thinking. Always remember, you are winning already just by starting the process.

The day-to-day planning is the process taking you ever closer to your weekly, 12-week and yearly goals. Consistency is everything. When you get the little areas right consistently, you can start to see the bigger changes happening.

How many times have you bulldozed through the day thinking, 'What do I need to do today, again?' or 'I really mustn't forget to do that!' You start something and then get interrupted, which really slows your progress. It's a frustrating way to live.

What you want to achieve is a routine that will allow you to look at your planner and know exactly what you have to do on any given day. It's your daily reference. It's there to stop you getting frustrated with trying to remember everything and being overwhelmed or angry with yourself when you get something wrong.

Having the daily plan in front of you allows you to wake up and focus on what you have to get done during the day.

Give it a skim during your morning and evening rituals to make sure you're all set and raring to go. If you are really well planned, you can break your day down further into hourly slots. I recommend you block out when very important things need to happen, otherwise you run the risk of your obligations eating up all your time again.

If you use an electronic calendar to back up your paper plan, you can block the same times out each week quickly and easily for things like date night. It makes it more difficult for colleagues to suggest awkward times for meetings – such as over lunch when you want to be in the gym – if you have already allocated that time slot.

Scheduling the same activities into the future also helps develop habits, routine and consistency.

 This really isn't hard work. It takes a few minutes to plan your day. How much better would you feel knowing exactly what you are doing and at what time? It gives you less to worry about and maintains a structure to your life.

Would that be of value to you? I am sure it would.

Daily planning provides the most accountability of all, of course. Nothing can slip for more than a day if you're reviewing your progress –

unless you tell yourself it's OK to let some stuff slip, which it isn't if you want to hit your yearly goals!

Accountability is vital. It's how you learn about the actions you are taking and highlights the things that are getting missed or neglected. A lot of the time you may not actually realise until the last minute that you overlooked something.

Having the tasks written down and instilling a review process in the evening allows you understand why some things never get accomplished but others do.

You can learn a lot about your strengths and weaknesses, which makes planning the next week, 12 weeks or year easier. You can anticipate problems much more effectively and come up with an alternative plan to solve it.

If you find that you are not following the plan and your week is all over the place, you know you have to be even more disciplined and focused on your "why".

What's the alternative? Keep doing the same shit you're doing now? How's that working for you? Badly, right? Yeah, some tough love but you can't afford to be sporadic with this.

It has to be a way of life!

THE BIG SUNDAY REVIEW AND PLAN SESSION

This is a method handed down from one of my mentors, Dan Meredith, in his book "How to be F*cking Awesome". (Read it, it's great!) His concept has helped me establish my take on Sunday night habits and I pass that structure on to others. The prioritisation tip is pure genius when it comes to simplifying your life to achieve more.

The best time to plan your week and the next seven days is over the weekend, preferably on Sunday evenings.

Saturdays are also good if you're new to planning and want to sleep on your plan and double-check it on Sunday with fresh eyes.

Getting clear in your mind about how you are going to accomplish everything you need to is reassuring. Making good choices throughout the week will be much easier when you know where you're headed.

Setting yourself up to win for the week starts with taking 20 to 30 minutes to schedule everything you have to do in the days ahead.

Start by sticking five minutes on the clock and jot down everything you want or need to do during the week. It doesn't matter what it is. The list doesn't need to be perfect. Simply concentrate on getting it down on paper. Some things will be related to your plan – those three gym sessions for example. Other tasks will be day-to-day chores like booking the car in for its annual service. That's fine, write that down too.

Once you have your list, prioritise your tasks into three categories

1. It *must* happen
2. It would be *good* if it happens
3. It can wait

Start by marking all the ones in your planner – everything that must happen. Make sure your ones genuinely reflect *your* priorities as you don't want those getting out of sync again and all those suffocating obligations that can wait.

Remember your priorities and actions must be in alignment to have a better quality of life – less worry, more fun.

Next add to your planner the most pressing of the twos if they can realistically be achieved in the time available without putting you under too much pressure. If, on reflection, some of those twos can wait then make them threes.

The threes can stay on the "some day" list until they become ones or twos. Alternatively you may decide to abandon them altogether or leave them for a quieter week on the horizon – it's your call.

Be wary of adding in twos and threes that matter more to other people than you – you need to be selfish with this. It's those sorts of habits that led to your life spiralling out of control before because you lost your focus.

Daily reviewing then becomes a lot easier as you can look at your schedule and make sure you're hitting those ones.

It's great to see all that consistent effort building up into something great.

TASK: CREATE YOUR YEARLY AND 12-WEEK PLANS

I have spoken in depth about the planning procedure and now it's time to use the 'I' from CICR – Implement – and get cracking on your plan.

Have a look at the worked examples in the resources section to get some ideas and the extra notes I have added to this task as a refresher. If you get stuck then reread the advice on how to complete each plan so you can be confident you've got it right.

TIP: You can post your plan in my free Facebook group to get some feedback. Alternatively, I can review your plan with you. See the "keep in touch" section for more advice.

What you are doing

I want you to decide on your four yearly goals – one for each area of your life – and check these goals are both feasible and ambitious.

Add these goals to your year plan. Then you'll need to break your goals down into your 12-week objectives and plan the first week for your first 12-week stint.

Don't plan all 12 weeks of your first quarter up front as you might need to tweak things after your daily and weekly reviews. It could be a big admin headache if you need to make a lot of changes. Concentrate on learning the process over that first week initially and then think about planning the weeks ahead.

After you've put your plan together, there is a second exercise to check it is watertight and will get you the results you want.

CHOOSE YOUR YEAR GOALS

The first step is to brainstorm everything and write down a series of potential goals for each area of your life

- personal development
- health

- professional life
- relationships

Remember to be ambitious and aim high to get the best results.

Once you've completed this process, review the list and pick your final favourite four big goals that work well together and provide the appropriate level of challenge.

Rule out any that mean you will

- limit yourself unduly by playing too small – *i.e. I will lose 12lbs this year*
- encounter a genuine reason why it cannot be attained – *i.e. I will lose 12st this year*

Once you're happy with your selection, start brainstorming how you will reach your goal. These are the potential stepping stones you will need.

Look for the things you need to complete early on as they are going to be added to your first quarter.

PLAN YOUR FIRST 12-WEEK BLOCK

Now look at those first 12 weeks in detail and put down what you will commit to achieving first over the three months. Remember, these will still be quite big stepping stones – more detail will come with your weekly and daily plans.

Roughly plan out the following three quarters to make sure your will hit your yearly goals.

Before you start your first weekly plan, it's time to check you've got your core yearly and 12-week targets right.

Let's give them a health check shall we?

TASK: HEALTH CHECKING YEARLY AND 12-WEEK PLANS

You may be getting excited at the thought of planning your life out, introducing structure and the new possibilities that await you. But remember you must learn to walk before you can run.

You need to review your plan to ensure it is not heading down a blind alley. You need to be 100 per cent sure implementing this plan will move you closer to your perfect day and remove the hassles and frustrations that have been plaguing you.

PRECISION

Your plan is not the place to generalise on things. Make sure you are super-specific when describing your objective.

Rather than saying you want to "lose weight", say *precisely* how much weight you want to lose. If you're going to learn a new language, will you be at a conversational level or become fluent in it?

You can't just say you want *new business*. How many additional customers do you want? What increase in revenue do you need? Want a new job? Write down what job you want, how many days a week it is and how much you want to be paid. You have to be specific! And the more detailed you are, the more likely you are to succeed.

You can't aim for vague goals. You need to be accurate to be able to track your progress.

MEASURABILITY

How are you going to track your progress against your plan? You can do this by using tick sheets to show each step being completed or scoring areas out of 10.

Incorporate a system that allows you to monitor progression. You want to see how you are doing on a regular basis to make sure your new positive habits are kicking in.

CHALLENGE

Are you testing your limits? You really can achieve anything you set your mind to, so give it your best shot – even if that means getting out of your comfort zone.

I am sure you're willing to work hard for some of the bigger things on your perfect day list. Reignite that fire in your belly, get out there and push yourself to do something amazing.

PRACTICALITY

Equally, be realistic. You want to be stretched, not overwhelmed with a plan that has left you with too much to do too soon.

Getting the balance is vital.

The biggest mistakes many make when planning is being too unrealistic. Giving yourself too much to do in the hope of getting it done quickly will result in you rushing your tasks and not doing things properly.

Be realistic about your life situation and whether you can achieve everything that you want to in the time-frame you have given yourself. Don't overwhelm yourself with it all because you will give up. You need to feel pleasantly challenged, not demoralised and defeated.

Seriously, if you've never managed a single session in the gym in the last 10 years, is six sessions a week for 52 weeks feasible? Not really.

Perhaps after a few months in when you have all the habits to go with it, but not from a standing start. It's just too much. More so if your three other big goals are equally ambitious.

Once the first quarter is out of the way you will have more experience and skill with your planning and be settled into your new routine. This is the time when you should start to think about stretching it a bit further.

MOTIVATION

You want a plan that drives you, and motivates you get out of bed and own the day. You have to be excited and inspired by your own goals for them to give you the motivation to get there.

If they aren't doing that, think about whether they really are the right goals. Is there a strong enough "why" behind your choice?

If you're not itching to make a start now, you'll really struggle in six months' time.

IMPORTANCE

If the goals that you are setting yourself are not truly meaningful then why would you set them?

Don't waste your time planning for things that really don't matter and instead just concentrate on the things that do.

Don't aim for something just because you can to impress people, like running a marathon. You have to really want to cross the finish line for yourself – not to show off.

Showing off about what a tough guy you are is not going to motivate you on a wet and dark Wednesday morning with a 12-mile training run ahead of you. Using the event to raise sponsorship for a charity close to your heart might.

Set your goals for the right reasons. Make sure they are meaningful to you in the long term, not just now as you fill out the planning paperwork.

TWEAKING YOUR PLAN

After giving your plan a health check, you might want to make changes. Here's some advice on how to improve yours.

Looking back at your self-audit, does your plan meet the requirements to solve your biggest issues right now? Fast-forward in your mind. Will the projected results from your plan fix the biggest problems that have stolen the joy from your life? Or is there something big you haven't addressed that will continue to be a thorn in your side?

Plans rarely ever go 100 per cent right first time, but don't panic. That's why you have the 'R for review' in your CICR formula, to check you're all set before heading off.

The worst thing you can do is follow another path that will not work.

Here are some suggestions…

FIXING PLAN PROBLEMS

When you can see your plan has got some holes in it, don't fret. It may be that you've set yourself too much to do or maybe you haven't planned in enough detail and your goals are starting to look like they clash.

You can't plan to spend more time with the family seeing a movie, have an early night for your morning gym session, attend your evening classes and be at the five-a-side match on the same night.

Something has to give.

Find the part of the plan that you are not happy with and change it. You can either refine it or start again, whichever you think will be easiest.

DISCUSS YOUR PLAN WITH SOMEONE ELSE

It is a really good idea to use a coach, partner or friends for accountability.

Talk them through how you see your plan working. They will have a fresh perspective and may offer you helpful advice along with their support.

Maybe the other person will make a plan too, and you can work towards your perfect day lifestyle together. That works well.

 You mustn't be closed about your plan. Express your thoughts and feelings to other people you're close too. Remember, the more you discuss things openly, the better those relationships become.

Once you're happy with your yearly and 12-week goals, it's time to map out your very first week. Exciting times are ahead of you my friend.

TASK: YOUR FIRST WEEK SCHEDULE AND DAY PLANS

Once you're happy that your plan is sound, it's time to map out the first week using the week and day planning sheets.

There is a space on the planner to jot down your objectives for each of the four areas of life. This time around these will be small and detailed steps, rather than big-picture things.

I recommend you have a look at the worked example as it's the easiest way to explain what's needed. There is a copy in the resources section.Also do the brain dump exercise so you can add in other "adulting" things that need doing, such as booking that dental appointment you thought about.

TASK: FOLLOW THE FIRST WEEK PLAN OBJECTIVES AND REVIEW THE RESULTS

Once your plan is put together, it's time to follow it for a week. Remember to review your progress and track how things go. You will learn a lot of valuable life lessons in your first week.

TASK: COMPLETE THE NEXT 11 WEEKS

Prepare your plans for each week for the rest of the 12-week block. setting putting your objective in for each of the 4 areas.

Keep these sheets safe because you'll be referring to them on a Sunday when you do your brain dump and fill in your daily tasks on your day planner.

HOW TO MAKE LIFE-LONG CHANGES SUCCESSFULLY

It is vital that you know how to make life-long changes if you are to avoid the temptation to return to your old ways.

Even with your new planning skills, some folks slip back into complacency.

People often fall off the CICR wagon because they lack discipline, commitment and consistency – three key ingredients for maintaining success.

 A great way to stay on track is to remember your "why" – your purpose and reason for making the changes in the first place. This will keep you moving forwards even when you are tempted to quit.

ACCEPT THAT FAILURE HAPPENS

It is best to go in with your eyes open and accept that you might fail at first when you implement your plan.

Just like a toddler learning to walk has a wobbly moment, the same might happen to you as you learn how to create your new lifestyle.

But just like the toddler, you need to pick yourself up again and have another go – without judgement and self-doubt – and you will improve.

It's important not to feel sorry for yourself if you fail. The secret is to instantly pick yourself up, dust yourself off and adapt. The longer you leave it the more likely you are to not do something about it.

Think of all the mistakes you've made in the past – you've survived, right? Mistakes are an inevitable part of learning and mastery. Like the saying goes, it's only a mistake if you've made it twice.

Look at the lead up to any successes or failures. What are the triggers? There will be clues that will enable you to understand why something did or didn't happen, so you can improve next time around.

For example: You read back in your planner that it's been a tough week at work and stress levels have been higher than normal. You notice your nutrition was poor at that time. Now this may have been triggered by getting home late and ordering a takeaway. Maybe you were distracted and forgot to take your lunch in with you and had a sausage roll and a can of pop from the convenience store instead. Everything has a trigger.

Look for the answers in your reviews and journal entries and make sure you take these into account in the long term.

BE GRATEFUL

Remember to reflect on the list of things you are grateful for. You will always be able to see some good things even among the biggest disappointments. It doesn't have to be all doom and gloom. Be positive, no matter what.

And do not give up when the going gets tough. You have to be patient with the process. It's natural to want to slip back into your old ways when you are low and the effort levels are high. Keep focused on what is improving – improvement is often just as important as achievement. You're in for the long game, right?

Resist the temptation to be defeatist and say, 'Nothing works for me'. This is the worst excuse in the world. If you have only been following your new structure for six weeks – to undo months or years of damage – then you simply have to be more patient.

Go back to the detailed self-audit, notice what is working and then build on that.

GET A CONTINGENCY PLAN

You are a proactive person now. Put together a contingency plan to handle any issues you can predict that could knock you off-kilter in advance.

Remember the scenario about going on an all-inclusive holiday for a fortnight and it conflicting with your fitness goals? There were workarounds, like taking the hiking tour up to the mountains or learning to windsurf, rather than sitting by the pool.

Look at all your options and make the best of your circumstances. The more you look, the easier it becomes to find answers to potential obstacles.

Plan how you will stay on track in advance. Have a few trusted fall backs. If you forget your lunch at work one day, pick up a pack of roast chicken from the convenience store to blunt your hunger rather than the king-size chocolate bar, sandwich and crisps meal deal. And work out a better reminder system for taking your food with you on work days, while you're at it!

This is a brilliant skill to develop so that when a curve ball hits, you're conditioned to deal with it and respond positively.

Aim to think ten steps ahead rather than two.

BUILD ON YOUR SUCCESSES

Look in your planner or journal for what has worked and see if you can apply something similar for another goal. What routines have helped you to get and stay on track? Is it getting shit done early in the morning? Perhaps it is attending 30-minute workout classes rather than hour-long  ones. Use what you already know works for you to boost your success going forward.

Review your planning sheets. You can't be expected to remember how every single day went over the course of a few months.

Look back at the activities that worked really well. It can easy to overlook your strengths. Refresh your memory as it will also boost your confidence.

BE EMPATHETIC WITH YOURSELF

When reviewing your plan and where things went wrong, ask yourself this question: Was it out of your control?

Don't stress about things you have no effect over. If your plan failed that day/week because of an external factor – such as the car breaking down making you late, a serious illness or death in the family – then it's likely that your plan is still OK. Chalk it up to experience. Dust yourself off and keep going.

DEVELOPING GOOD HABITS MAKES IT EASIER

When you implement habit and routine you become a lot more consistent with your planning and execution.

Do you brush your teeth without thinking about it? Of course you do. Going for a beer Friday night or having dinner at the table are habits and routines people do without even thinking.

The more you work towards your plan, the more likely you are to be on the ball with keeping good habits on autopilot. It will start to become a way of life – a routine.

HOW TO BOOST YOUR CHANCES OF SUCCESS

Commitment, implementation, consistency and reviewing are the keys to your success. Whatever you do in life; live by the CICR formula.

If something isn't working then it's likely that one of these areas is slipping. You have to be pretty honest with yourself and sometimes it's hard to face the fact you are falling down on one or more of them.

Pay attention and do your best to pre-empt issues. It's much easier to nip a problem in the bud than let it build and have a crisis to resolve.

 If you feel yourself struggling, remember your commitment is founded by your "why". The why is most likely the reason that you committed to a new way of life in the first place.

You should write your why down and put it everywhere. The more reminders you see about why you're doing what matters to you, the easier it is to stay motivated. It definitely boosts commitment and consistency.

Drill down further and list all the reasons your why is so important to you. The more you dig into your thoughts, values and beliefs, the more you are able to draw strength from them.

They act like a tree's roots, giving it the strength to stay firm even in the strongest of gales.

REWARD YOURSELF FOR PROGRESS

This process can be draining. Living far outside your comfort zone can be frightening, confusing and tiring. Make time to reward yourself for your efforts or life can easily become one big, long grind.

Choose rewards that will make you feel good and boost your results. For example, rather than rewarding yourself with a massive takeaway at the end of a week, why not spend the money on some new gym gear? Or maybe see that film you always wanted to on Netflix? How about a long walk in the countryside with your partner and spending some quality time with them?

Have small and regular rewards for each stepping stone you reach. Treat yourself to bigger ones for hitting your 12-week and yearly goals. Make the reward size match the size of your achievement.

Decide what your rewards will be in advance. That way, you can put pictures up as a reminder of how good it will be when you've earned them. This technique can also join your "why" in helping to keep you motivated.

TEST AND ADJUST YOUR PLAN

Just like a crew on a sailing boat trims the sails as they make progress to stay on course, you need to do so with your plan.

Keep an eye on your circumstances, your results, your goals and learn from what's going on.

Perhaps you got a bit trigger happy in planning your morning routine and squeezed too many things into your golden hour. Maybe that made your "you time" rushed rather than relaxed.

Think about ways to tweak it to improve. Perhaps instead of prepping your food for the day in the morning you could do it the night before?

Focus on continual improvement and you will be rewarded.

AVOID PREJUDGING HOW THINGS WILL GO

Sometimes you just have to put faith in your plan. It's natural to feel like you might be biting off more than you can chew – especially when you have gone for those big goals.

But don't let defeatism creep into your thinking. Your weekly plan should break big tasks down into small, easy stepping stones that get you to where you want to be.

Focus on how simple those next steps are to make you feel more positive about what you're doing.

The steps were manageable when you health-checked your plan and they will be manageable when you're doing them.

LOOK FOR ANSWERS IN OTHER PEOPLE'S SUCCESS

Look at what successful people are doing and how they got to where they are today.

You will have heard the phrase, 'You don't need to reinvent the wheel'. Why not take inspiration from someone else that has solved part of your puzzle already? It will save you a few hard yards and you could learn from their mistakes

There are lots of places you can find this inspiration.

Books are an obvious choice. They are full of someone else's knowledge and wisdom that can help you out on your journey. I wrote this book because I learned how to take charge of my life and decided to share my story with you. Think about what you want to do and find a book to help.

Podcasts are also brilliant for offering knowledge and advice. The great thing about podcasts is you can often do something else at the same time as listening. You could be out running or commuting while listening to great points of views at the same time. It's a win-win scenario.

DOCUMENT YOUR PROGRESS

Keeping a record of your progress is such a powerful way to watch your journey unfold. It's a good idea to cross off your daily tasks as you complete them. It's very satisfying knowing another stepping stone has been reached and you are another step closer to the big prize.

The minute you have completed that workout or finished that book, you can go ahead and cross it off your list.

This is guaranteed to boost your motivation and your mood. The enthusiasm this creates makes the next step that little bit easier and motivating.

SHARE YOUR WHY

Speaking to other people about your motivations will really clarify why you do anything. It's interesting to see what drives other people too.

Have you ever told anyone your "why" or the reason behind why you're doing what you're doing? Perhaps you are losing weight because one of your mates had a laugh about your size and it sparked a reaction. Maybe you have had a calling to take up a new career, rather than settle with the job you fell into?

Tell the world. It will reinforce your purpose every day.

SEEK OUT AN ACCOUNTABILITY PARTNER

When it gets tough or when you just want to talk about the change process, it really helps to have somebody to call upon.

This is where having an accountability partner is effective.

They are likely to be on their own journey so you can help and encourage each other along. It's likely you will both fall into a slump at some point – but not at the same time. This means you can help offer each other support.

See if your accountability partner has similar "whys" or plans you can relate to. If you can work on something directly together, again your chance of success is boosted.

It's great to get together with people you have common ground with such as other dads or work colleagues. Being around people with the same positive mindset, purpose and goals can be priceless during difficult times.

WHAT TO DO AFTER YOUR FIRST 12-WEEK PLAN

The answer is simple. You do a detailed review of how it went, of course. You will have gained massive experience and must now learn to use that for the next 12 weeks of your programme. Were your goals met? Did you overstretch yourself or did you not set the bar high enough?

HAVE A WEEK OFF

As wonderful as it is to make massive change, remember you are still new to this. You don't want to burn out and get overloaded when you're just getting started. If you feel exhausted then you will not make good decisions.

Take a breather so that you can take in all you have achieved in the first 12 weeks. Reflect on the successes and the failures. Compare your life now to how it looked 12 weeks ago.

And arrange a few of those rewards I suggested you set your heart on.

REFLECT ON YOUR SUCCESSES

This has two benefits. Firstly, you can be fully aware of what works for you and keep doing it. What's more, you can look for ways to do those things even better – further efficiencies.

Use this feedback to make informed decisions about next 12 weeks. Now you have your planning skills to help you, could you set a bigger goal for the next quarter?

REPEAT THE DETAILED LIFE AUDIT

It's a good idea to use your down-time during this week off to do another life audit. The things that are working and not working will have changed this time. That will tend to mean different activities making it onto your new weekly plan.

It's a good idea to review your yearly plan too. Is it still in alignment with how you want life to be? Were you a bit cautious at the start and could dream a little bigger now? Or were you overly optimistic and need to be a little less ambitious if you are to hit your weekly targets?

Remember to review and adjust.

CONGRATULATIONS

You are now well on the way to becoming the best possible version of you. You are starting your second 12-week block.

Do let me know how you're getting on. I know how dark life can get at times. Well done for committing to changing your lot.

I'd love to hear about how much you are enjoying your new life.

James

RECOMMENDED READING AND PODCASTS

This is a list of resources I found helpful as I deepened my understanding in the four key areas of my life. They are perfect for your golden hour or your commute.

Books

Knight, Sarah. *Get Your Sh*t Together*, Quercus Editions, 2016

Carnegie, Dale. *How To Win Friends & Influence People*, Cedar, 1998

Keppe, Norberto R. *The Origin Of Illness*, Campbell Hall Press, 2002

Podcasts

James Boardman, *Fitness It's a State Of Mind*, iTunes, 2016

Jamie Alderton, *Mindset With Muscle*, iTunes, 2015

Gary Vaynerchuk, *The GaryVee Audio Experience*, iTunes

Dan Meredith and Jamie Alderton, *The Body and The Beast*, iTunes

Tony Robbins, *The Tony Robins Experience*, iTunes

RESOURCES

Below are examples of how to fill out your audit and planning sheets. I find reviewing some examples really help the penny drop for people.

You can download a set of blank and sample worksheets here: http://boardmanjames.com/book-resources

LIFE AUDIT SHEET

This sheet is broken down into two columns. These are headed 'Working' and 'Not working'. Under working, you are going to brain dump all the things that are working for you for each of the four areas of life. You will do exactly the same for not working; brain-dump all of the things that don't work for you. Put them down in any order.

You have to be brutal with your life audit score. There is no point lying or burying your head in the sand and thinking that things are better than they really are. The more honest you are the more likely you will be able to turn things around.

Completing this form helps you to work out what you want to do more of and what you need to do less of. You'll find that the self-audit forms will open your eyes to how you're living your life right now, and where and why some things are falling short.

Life audit sheet

Personal development	Score 3
Working	**Not working**
Listen to weekly podcast	Learning but not implementing
Being proactive about socialising, networking	Low esteem during social events, nervous, low confidence.
Reading self-help books	Not applying what I learn
Noticing things to be grateful for	Once in a bad mood all my good habits go out the window.
Very organised at work	No structure to leisure time
Have some consistent habits, brushing teeth, eating breakfast	Other habits not sticking, poor consistency.

REMEMBERING YOU SHEET

This worksheet helps you get in touch with who you were and who you wanted to be at different times of your life. It can help you decide what you want to do in future.

Remembering you sheet

30 +	30 -
Birth of first child	Hated long working hours
Honeymoon in Barbados	Strapped for cash

PLANNER WORKED EXAMPLE

I have created a basic example of how you can put the theories of the book in a practical format.

As I spoke about in the book, I have set out my yearly goals. I have kept things simple here, but you can go into much more detail as you brain-dump the next 12 months. Then you can break down the process further.

On the next page is an example yearly goals sheet.

YEARLY GOALS

Use this sheet to store the big things you want to aim for in the next 12 months.

Yearly goals sheet	
Personal development	I will consistently use weekly planning to make space in my life to do what I want, rather than firefight.
Health	I want to lose 4st over the year, and become much fitter and stronger. I want to eat better and only have one takeaway a month as a treat
Professional life	I want to get a professional certification so I can get a promotion at work
Relationships	I want to spend • a week on a dream holiday with family • all weekend with the kids • a short break with my parents • 6 go-karting days with the guys • 5 minutes a week thanking each of my team for the great job they do

POSSIBLE SOLUTIONS SHEET

Use this sheet to store possible ways to solve problems and meet your goals.

Possible solutions sheet

Goal name: Adding structure to life	Priority
Do my daily journaling	
Read recommended books – one book a month	
Get an accountability partner	
Commit to the 'golden hour'	
Tracking progress	
Be around like-minded individuals, who have common goals	
Join the local college for a meditation course	
Choose relevant audio books and podcasts that will good for commute	
Print out my 'why' reminders	
Print out my weekly plan and carry it with me	

12-WEEK PLAN SHEET

The 12-week goals allow you to break down the yearly goals into smaller actions you need to take. This form gives you an example of how that is done when it comes to you making your goals.

12-week plan sheet

	List what you need to do in priority order	Done
1	Stick to having my daily golden hour	☐
2	Lose 1st in weight with a personal trainer	☐
3	Get book on Excel and learn 2 skills a week	☐
4	Be home for dinner with the kids	☐

	Why are you doing it?
1	Gives me structure and a plan
2	I need advice and accountability. If I pay, I will do it
3	Get quicker with Excel and enjoy using it more
4	To have a closer relationship with children

	How does this help you move forwards?
1	Gives me space to focus on my priorities
2	If I don't turn up I will let the trainer down and waste my money plus I won't lose the weight I want to
3	I am more productive so I don't have to stay late
4	They are my why – plus being fitter means I can ride a bike or play football with them at weekends

WEEKLY PRIORITIES AND PLAN SHEETS

The weekly plan sheet examples below identify your priorities for the week. It also allows you to plan your week so that you can focus on the tasks that will take you forward and improve your life. By completing the forms it will allow you to become much more proactive.

Week one priorities

	List what you need to do in the four life areas	Planned
1	Listen to a helpful podcast daily	☐
2	Get three workouts in	☐
3	Get some Excel for beginners tuition	☐
4	Putting the kids to bed each night	☐

Weekly plan sheet

	Monday	Tuesday	Wednesday	Thursday	Friday	Saturday	Sunday	Score
PD	Golden hour	Golden hour	Golden hour	Golden hour	Golden hour	Golden hour	Planning next week	10
H	Ask for recommendations for PT	Check their websites and choose who I like best	Call trainer	Brisk walking	Brisk walking	Visit trainer for initial consultation	Rest	9
PL	Find Excel book on Amazon and order it	Look for some tutorials YouTube	Read a chapter on the train	Practice what I read at lunchtime	Rest	Rest	Rest	10
R	Leave on time	Leave on time	Leave on time	Leave on time	Leave on time	2-hour walk with kids	Rest	7
PD	Review & gratitude	Review & gratitude	Review & gratitude	Review & gratitude	Review & gratitude	Review & gratitude	Double check plan	

KEEP IN TOUCH

This book shouldn't be the beginning and end of our relationship. I don't want you to read this and just lose touch. Let's keep this going. I genuinely want to help you.

I've got lots of other things to share with you to help.

JOIN MY FREE FACEBOOK GROUP

Addressing the long-running problems in your life can be a lonely business at times. I certainly find it easier to be surrounded by people with the same goals to talk to, learn from, support and enjoy the journey with.

It really helps me stick with it when I don't feel like it.

That's why I have created this group, JB Fitness Group – to give you extra support and camaraderie as you change your life. Please join as it will help you.

https://www.facebook.com/groups/1757972844489690/

After joining, take time to read the pinned post. This includes advice on how to get most out of the group, where to introduce yourself and links to further resources that will help you.

When you post your introduction, remember to include what your goals are. You'll find other guys that are in a similar position and may be able to find an accountability partner, a friendly ear, or some helpful insights.

This is a great platform to share your successes as well as losses. It's similar to having a journal – but one that will give you support and advice back. You'll be surprised at how motivational it can be to you and others in the group.

NEWSLETTER

My newsletter is distributed three times a week. It includes lots of ideas that will help your health, fitness and wellness.

It includes workouts, training advice, healthy tasty recipes, examples of habit building, and much more. You can sign up for the newsletter on the home page on here:

www.boardmanjames.com

NEED MORE HELP FROM ME

Even when you know what you need to do, sometimes you still need extra help. If that sounds like you, please reach out and ask. It doesn't matter where you are in the world, thanks to the power of the internet we can work together.

Over the years, I have put together ways to help guys become the best version of themselves.

21 DAY 'KICK START' ONLINE PROGRAMME

The 21 day 'KICK START' Programme is a fat-burning programme lasting 3 weeks. There are 15 powerful bodyweight-based workout routines, which can be done anywhere, at home or away.

Without going too deep into the science, HIIT (high-intensity interval training) fitness routines are the most effective method of burning body fat while building muscle at the same time.

The programme will build your self-esteem and confidence as well as develop a healthy and balanced lifestyle.

Visit:
http://boardmanjames.com/21-day-kick-start-programme

COACHING AT THE JB ACADEMY

I'm a huge believer in accountability and I love to work personally with others to help them live the life they want.

The JB Academy offers group coaching and accountability. As well as extra resources such as fitness technique and education to improve your fitness performance, there are regular nutrition ideas and guidance.

We also hold regular Q&A sessions in the group so that you get the best advice possible when you need it.

You can find out full details at
www.boardmanjames.com

THE STATE OF MIND PLANNER

I have put together a printed planner to go with this book. It's a convenient way to keep your plan sheets together and store them over time. It's also a good way to get "hard" copies if you don't have easy access to a printer.

CONTACT ME

If there's anything else you'd like to ask or tell me, you can email me directly and I will personally reply:
me@boardmanjames.com